DOCTOR in the HOUSE

A Physician-Turned-Congressman Offers His Prescription for Scrapping Obamacare— and Saving America's Medical System

Congressman
MICHAEL C. BURGESS, MD

WND Books

Doctor in the House

WND Books

Published by WorldNetDaily

Washington, D.C.

Copyright © 2011
Michael C. Burgess

WND Books are distributed to the trade by:
Midpoint Trade Books
27 West 20th Street, Suite 1102
New York, NY 10011

WND Books are available at special discounts for bulk purchases. WND Books, Inc. also publishes books in electronic formats. For more information call (541) 474-1776 or visit www.wndbooks.com.

First Edition

ISBN 13 Digit: 978-1-936488-25-4

Library of Congress information available

Printed in the United States of America

10 9 8 7 6 5 4 3 2 1

TABLE OF CONTENTS

FOREWORD

by Speaker Newt Gingrich

At a time when America is at a crossroads about what kind of health system we should have, Congressman Michael Burgess has written a very important explanation of politics, policy, patients, and physicians.

This book is a remarkable essay on life, medicine, health care, politics, and Congress. It's so much more interesting and so much richer in human experience than most health policy books that I recommend it to every American.

When I began reading Congressman Burgess' essay, I thought I knew him. We had worked on a number of health care issues. He was clearly hard working, intelligent, enthusiastic, and a dedicated conservative. He was also courageous and willing to take on the power structure of both political parties.

Little did I realize the depth of his personal human experiences.

This book carries us back to his grandfather's role as a famous medical doctor in Canada two generations ago. We learn about the rise of government dominated bureaucratic medicine in Canada and his father's decision, while studying at the Mayo Clinic, to stay in the United States in order to have the freedom to do the right thing for his patients no matter what the government bureaucrats wanted done.

The roots of Congressman Burgess' opposition to government dictated bureaucratic health care can be found in his family's history long before the rise of Obamacare. His patriotism becomes clear in his reaction to the terrorist attacks of 9/11 and his compulsion to do something for his country.

The opportunity created by Majority Leader Dick Armey's decision to retire created a moment of choice and self definition for the doctor. He ran a grassroots campaign that got him into a runoff and then into Congress.

From doctor to congressman turned into an odyssey of learning in its own right. Every American will find themselves better informed about the problems of congressional government after reading this candid and thoughtful memoir.

As America wrestles with big decisions in health, deficits, job creation, national security, and a host of other challenges, Congressman Burgess is going to play a bigger and bigger role.

This book gives you a real insight into the passion and commitment he will bring to the struggle for successful self government and the extension of freedom.

DOCTOR in the HOUSE

CHAPTER ONE

TOWN HALL TENSION

THE SUN HAD BARELY RISEN ABOVE THE TREE LINE TO MY LEFT AS I made my way along historic U.S. 377 toward the heart of Denton, Texas. Old 377 runs alongside U.S. 77 and, in the days before the Interstate highway system, ran right up through the heartland of America, connecting Brownsville, Texas at the Rio Grande with Sioux Falls, South Dakota—with ten thousand wheat fields in between. Today it was connecting me to one of the most important meetings of my political career.

It was early August and North Texas was in the middle of an extended string of cloudless 100-plus degree days. I was uncomfortable as I drove, but not because of the rising temperature. Frankly, I was just nervous. As the fourth-term Republican Congressman for Texas' 26th District, I was on my way to do a town hall meeting in one of my district's largest cities. Denton, which lies about thirty miles north of Dallas and Fort Worth, was my boyhood home. I had always found it to be friendly territory, but today I was heading into what I knew would be a buzz saw of constituent emotion. It was America's "Summer of Discontent" and across the country passions had been rising faster than the temperatures.

I was keenly aware that in the previous forty-eight hours a number of my congressional colleagues in both political parties, freshly home after the August recess, had encountered large, rowdy crowds and angry questions at what were ordinarily sleepy, sparsely attended little community meetings.

Indeed, I had seen the national news reports two days earlier. Democrat Kathy Castor's town hall in Tampa, Florida had quickly devolved into a rowdy shouting match between opponents and a few advocates of a government-mandated overhaul of America's health care system as more than a thousand people showed up for a meeting in a hall that only accommodated 250. There, an already tense situation became more volatile when individuals carrying union ID cards were allowed into the meeting through a side entrance. This was after hundreds of non-union constituents were turned away.

I had also read reports of how John Dingell's meeting in Romulus, Michigan had drawn a huge, vocal crowd—more than 600 people showed for a meeting in a room with a capacity of 150—a throng that was clearly in no mood to sit passively and listen to evasive political spin and vague platitudes. Dingell was a lead author of the Democrats' health care legislation in the House. In the middle of the raucous event, an older man wheeled his cerebral palsy-stricken son to the very front of the room and loudly challenged Dingell about his legislation amid cheers and chants from the crowd. The image was carried by wire services to newspapers and Websites nationwide. Reports of similar fireworks were coming in from all over the country.

Closer to home, I was also aware that just the day before, Representative Pete Sessions who, like me, represents a portion of the Dallas-Fort Worth "Metroplex," had filled to overflowing an 800-seat civic center in nearby Richardson, Texas. I had spoken with Pete afterwards. He said that in 12-plus years of serving in Congress he'd never seen his constituents so animated and alarmed about an issue. He told me to expect hard questions and deeply frustrated people at my meeting. Further, he warned—they are not interested in hearing you talk; you are to listen to them.

Believe me, I took him seriously. For the Denton town hall meeting of August 8, 2009, we acquired the biggest venue we could—a meeting room in the Center for the Visual Arts that would accommodate about 400 chairs with room for another 100 people willing to stand around the perimeter of the room. Anticipating the possibility of even more people than that, my staff planned to set up speakers and microphones out in the parking lot, just in case. I knew it was going to be an "interesting" event.

The fact is, I had already had a taste of town hall intensity over the brief Fourth of July recess a month earlier when, to my shock, between 250 and 300 people showed up on a holiday to express concern and vent real anger about the "Cap and Trade" legislation that Speaker Nancy Pelosi had just rammed through the House over objections and "no" votes by conservatives like me.

To understand my surprise, you have to know that in my few years of experience as a Congressman, these town hall get-togethers had always been pretty intimate affairs—like my very first town hall after being elected in 2002.

At that time, I was brand new to the whole business of representing a congressional district and I was leaning heavily on those more experienced and the Republican leadership to guide me and help me avoid pitfalls. As I flew home Friday evening for my very first Saturday morning town hall meeting in Keller, Texas, I was armed with talking points and a speech I had been handed by the House Republican leadership office.

When I showed up the next morning for the meeting, there was a grand total of one person in attendance. That one individual happened to be the mayor of Keller who most likely felt obligated to show up for the new Congressman's first official meeting in her city. Another person wandered in about halfway through the allotted time. Not knowing what else to do, I pressed ahead and delivered my speech!

In the years that followed, attendance at these events grew—crowds of thirty or forty people were commonplace—but not by much. That's what made that Fourth of July recess of 2009 so startling.

The vote on the Waxman-Markey legislation—a misguided attempt at a global warming response widely known as the "Cap and Trade" bill — passed, but only narrowly: 219-212. Eight Republicans voted for the bill, while forty-four Democrats voted against it. I was one of the "no" votes and for many good reasons, chief among them that the bill amounted to a major tax increase on average Americans who would end up paying more for energy and fuel, should the bill become law. The bill, in my opinion, would result in massive economic disruptions for our nation while making a negligible dent in worldwide carbon emissions.

The final vote on Cap and Trade didn't take place until late Friday night, right before we adjourned for the July 4th recess, so we all missed our flights home for the short break. I was scheduled to do a town hall meeting in Keller Saturday morning at 10:00 a.m. and managed to catch a 6:00 a.m. flight that got me into Dallas-Fort Worth in just enough time to catch my breath and head to the event. I expected, at most, the usual two- or three-dozen constituents. Given that it was the weekend before the Fourth of July, I wondered if anyone would show up at all. I couldn't believe what I found when I arrived.

The parking lot was overflowing with cars and the meeting room was packed. City officials were scrambling to open up ancillary rooms to accommodate the crowd. The Fire Marshall had been called in to make sure no codes were violated. And the mood of those in attendance was very different from the sleepy, low-key tone I usually encountered.

The House vote on Waxman-Markey was barely twelve hours old but people were deeply upset about what they'd seen on the news the night before. They couldn't believe that a majority of representatives in Congress could have agreed to do to the American people what that legislation would clearly do. Like the grassroots passion over health care legislation, this wasn't manufactured outrage or organized window-dressing for the media. There was no media. There was just this spontaneous, broad-based anger about growing government size and escalating burdens of taxation and regulation on individuals and businesses. And if I thought having voted the "right" way would fully exempt me from that anger, I quickly learned otherwise.

A falling tide lowers all ships, it seems. So as corruption scandals enveloped high profile Democrats like Charles Rangel—and as each day seemingly produced an alarming new proposal to regulate, tax or ban something—the approval ratings for the Nancy Pelosi-led Congress continued to fall from their already historic lows.

To many of these understandably distraught citizens, Congress was the problem, and I was a member of Congress. Facing that frustration got uncomfortable at times. I quickly discovered that I couldn't just shrug my shoulders and say, "Hey, I'm on your side on this."

As much anger as I was facing, my colleagues on the other side of the aisle were quickly starting to dread the very words "town hall." With Democrats fully in charge in both houses of Congress and in possession of the White House, they had the political wherewithal to pass pretty much anything they wanted. And what they had been wanting for decades was a massive restructuring of the way health care is delivered, priced, and paid for in America. What they clearly had not counted on, however, was a widespread, spontaneous grassroots uprising among Americans who ordinarily only think about politics every two to four years.

Of course, there were many on the Democratic side and in the Left-leaning media who asserted (and may have actually believed) that these throngs of distressed and angry citizens descending upon these town hall meetings represented anything but a spontaneous wave of public opinion. Accusations quickly flew that my fellow Republicans, or perhaps the major health insurance companies, had somehow orchestrated and facilitated these turnouts. The cry of "astroturfing" was commonly heard—a euphemism used in political activist circles to describe the cynical act of busing in loyal supporters to make it appear to television news cameras that a given cause has broad, deep public support. Astroturf appears to be real grass from a distance, but it's not the real thing.

I knew that the astroturfing charge was nonsense. For one thing, I was painfully conscious that we Republicans were utterly disorganized and behind the curve in developing a response to the various pieces of sweeping legislation being crafted on Capitol Hill. Since being sworn in, the new administration and the Democratic leadership in both houses of Congress had been generating budget-busting expansions of federal power faster than we could track and process them. When it came to mobilizing the base, focusing pressure on lawmakers, and putting passionate interest groups on public display for television cameras, we Republicans were worse than rank amateurs. That's called "community organizing" and it's the other side that has developed it into a high art form. In fact, a former community organizer was now occupying the Oval Office and was the chief proponent of much of that new legislation.

On the other hand, the people I met represented every class, race, age, and walk of life. They defied stereotyping. What they had in common was anger.

They didn't want to hear me talk about process. They didn't want to hear me explain how we were in the minority and how limited our power was in committee. They didn't want to hear about my great amendments that never saw the light of day. All they wanted to know was what they could do to get out there and stop the runaway freight train of government spending.

In light of those conversations, I talked to the Republican leadership on several occasions throughout the summer about what I was hearing and seeing back home—that concerned citizens were asking for a plan of action but we didn't have one to give them.

Right before we left for the August recess, House Minority Leader John Boehner stood up in our conference meeting and said, "When you all get back we're going to have some plans and initiatives for you that will help you put some of this grassroots passion to work." I remember thinking at the time, "Too late! We missed it." This, of course, is what makes the frequent charges of astroturfing so ridiculous. We weren't leading our constituents. They were leading us! As further evidence, Republicans who were already on record as being strongly opposed to the type of legislation being proposed were just as likely to see their town hall meetings swarmed with distressed constituents as were Democrats in favor of it.

No, the waves of grassroots anger that swelled and broke across the nation in August of 2009 were genuine and born of conversations around the water cooler and over the back fence rather than, as many critics charged, robotic obedience to AM talk radio. Plans to radically alter the structure of the health care system had clearly touched a nerve.

It was this knowledge, combined with the lessons learned at my July town halls, that was the source of my nervousness as I prepared for that

August 8 town hall in Denton. I had joked about my apprehension with
a friend the night before, "I know we're going to have a big crowd," I told
him. "I'm just not sure whether I'm walking into a county fair or a public
stoning."

My concern was eased a bit by the knowledge that the ones getting
the worst of it across the country were the liberal Democrats who were
on record as being in favor of a radical overhaul of the health care system.
Ironically, the very politicians being shouted down by packed meeting
rooms filled with exasperated voters were the same folks who had previously warned me and my conservative colleagues that we would live to regret
our opposition to a progressive government takeover of health care. "You're
going to pay a high political price if you oppose us on this," we were told.
"The people want this." "You're on the wrong side of history," one legislator
told me. Another bluntly said, "We won. Get over it."

I had left home at daybreak—several hours before the planned starting
time that morning--because I wanted to get there plenty early to make sure
the logistics of crowd management were in place, to greet people as they
arrived, and to hopefully mingle a bit. Furthermore, the last thing I wanted
was the visual spectacle of me "arriving" after a huge crowd had already
gathered.

As I approached the historic heart of downtown, the blue Romanesque
Revival domes of Denton County's Courthouse-on-the-Square came into
view. Like many of Texas' grand old cities, Denton was laid out with a large
public square at the very center of town—upon which sits a piece of archi-
tecture as impressive as the former courthouse.

The site of the meeting that morning, the Center for the Visual Arts,
was several blocks east of the town square. Nevertheless, it seemed that
every parking spot in the downtown area was already occupied. Signs were
in place on every street corner directing drivers to parking lots around the
downtown area. Buses were shuttling people from the parking areas to the
meeting site. I could see that early arrivers had already grabbed all 400
seats in the air-conditioned building and the remaining standing room was
filling rapidly.

As the official start time for the meeting approached, police were estimating that more than a thousand other individuals were standing in the parking lot directly outside the building. A fortunate few found shade under the live oak trees at the perimeter of the lot. But most stood in the glare and heat of an August sun that was climbing high in the sky.

I chose to speak outside where the majority of the crowd was located. The crowd was rowdy but in a good-natured, almost festive way. There had been several days of national media coverage about the town halls during which many people had heard town hall attendees described as "angry mobs" and "right wing extremists." A few days earlier Speaker Nancy Pelosi went so far as to tell an interviewer: "I think they're Astroturf... You be the judge. They're carrying swastikas and symbols like that to a town meeting on healthcare." Of course, Speaker Pelosi's off-the-cuff accusation makes no sense. If, as some Democrats asserted, these crowds showing up at town halls were nothing more than carefully crafted props for political theater— if they were just pawns of the health insurance lobby—then they certainly wouldn't be displaying swastikas or other inflammatory symbols. And if they were all right-wing extremist kooks, then they weren't the well-dressed corporate shills and country club elites that other critics had painted them to be. Speaker Pelosi's charge that these profoundly concerned citizens were simultaneously "Astroturf" and "carrying swastikas" was absurd and insulting.

Such characterizations had clearly struck a nerve with many of the folks that came out that Saturday morning. I saw lots of signs that made satirical reference to all the negative media reports, including one taped to the t-shirt of a smiling silver-haired gentleman in shorts and sneakers. It read: "I'm a proud member of the angry mob."

The sudden media focus on the town halls also activated those who were in favor of the various Democratic proposals being put forth. Several pro-health care reform groups had encouraged their members to turn out for this event, including The League of Women Voters and Planned Parenthood. Nevertheless, my seat-of-the-pants estimate, and that of several other neutral observers, was that roughly 80 percent of the crowd was opposed to the current proposals and about 20 percent seemed to be in favor.

I kept my opening remarks brief and emphasized that the purpose of the event was to allow me to hear from my constituents, not the other way around. I had instructed my staff to make sure that, if possible, we got just as many questions or statements from individuals who supported the legislation as we did those who opposed it. And even though opponents outnumbered proponents roughly four-to-one, we succeeded in achieving that balance.

As I mentioned, the crowd was rowdy and vocal. And given the composition of this assembly, it was no surprise that when someone expressed opposition to the health care bill or voiced concern about another Obama-Pelosi initiative, there were loud cheers and applause in addition to a few "boos." When a supporter of the measure spoke, there was usually a smattering of applause and a wave of groans, "boos," and murmurs. But no one was shouted down. Everyone who got to the microphone got to have his or her say. And I didn't see or hear about any instances of people getting in each other's faces or shouting at one another. In fact, I noticed that one young gentleman with long hair and Birkenstock sandals who held up a sign that read "I'm FOR socialized medicine" was unchallenged, unmolested and viewed as a bit of a curiosity by the flag-waving, flag-wearing crowd.

In the end, the event bore more of a resemblance to the county fair than the public execution I had feared.

That day in August proved to be more than just a nerve-wracking, though fascinating encounter with democracy in action for me. It also seems to have changed the course of my legislative career. Numerous attendees had shot videos of the event that ended up on You Tube and then virally circulated around the country via the Internet. Higher awareness of the fact that I had spent almost three decades as a physician before entering Congress suddenly gave me a platform to share my ideas about what *real* health care reform should look like.

From that day forward, I have had more and wider opportunities to share my ideas and perspectives about health care in America. With humbling frequency, I have been asked my opinion about the volatile intersection of government and medicine. In the intervening days I have found myself squinting into television lights while fielding questions about end-of-life counseling, Medicare, public option insurance, malpractice suits, and myriad other issues. And if my voice seems to be carrying a touch more weight at this moment in history, perhaps it is because, out of the 535 men and women who comprise the House and Senate of the United States, I am among a handful of those who have been practicing physicians.

You see, prior to becoming the underdog winner of a vacant House seat in 2002 . . . prior to becoming the founder and first chairman of the Congressional Health Care Caucus . . . I spent almost thirty years delivering babies in and around Dallas, Texas. Before I was the "Honorable" Michael C. Burgess, I was just "Doctor B" to a generation of North Texans—an OB-GYN with an additional Masters Degree in Medical Management.

I believe that background has uniquely prepared to me to bring clarity and common sense to the perplexing national debate over health care. On the pages that follow, that's what I hope to do.

CHAPTER TWO

OUT OF CANADA

WHEN I WAS GROWING UP, EVERYONE ASSUMED I WOULD PURSUE MEDICINE. After all, my father was a doctor, as was his father before him. Perhaps that's why I was cool to the idea early on. It's no secret that teenagers are wired by nature to resist anything that adults uniformly consider a good idea. I came around eventually, however, surrendered to genetic predisposition, and went to med school.

I never knew my grandfather, but he was a widely respected physician who taught Obstetrics and Gynecology at McGill University's medical school in Montreal, Canada. (Yes, this Texas country doctor has roots in Canada!) My grandfather practiced medicine in Canada back in a time when doctors there could still enjoy some financial rewards for all their years of study and sacrifice—back before every doctor and nurse became a government employee by virtue of their country's "single payer" health care system. He invested well, too; traveled the world; became a collector of art; and was well thought of in Montreal society. Then, like so many, he lost nearly everything in the Great Depression.

Not too long ago I came across my grandfather's obituary as it appeared in the 1940 Canadian Journal of Nursing. It was moving and humbling to see how revered and respected he was by those who had worked with him—especially the nurses.

My father was born in Montreal, was an only child and, following in his father's steps, entered medical school in the early 1940s—just as World War II was starting. He also joined the Canadian Navy about the same time.

After the war he completed his internship and went right into general practice. It was there that he somehow found himself assigned to practice in Noranda, Quebec—a tiny mining village in the Canadian wilderness nearly 400 miles northwest of Montreal. For the city-raised son of a prominent doctor-professor, it had to feel a lot like being sent to Siberia. Around that time he met and married my mother.

There is much I don't know about those years and the circumstances that led my father to make some major changes. He passed away in 2005, and I miss him. And I wish he were here now to fill in some of these blanks for me. What I do know is that he sensed the winds of change blowing where the practice of medicine in Canada was concerned. It was right about this time that the first government health insurance proposals were emerging on a rising tide of socialist sentiment. Whatever the reasons, my father hadn't been practicing in Noranda very long before he started applying for residencies in hospitals south of the Canadian border. My father was looking to move himself and his new bride to the United States.

He got his opportunity when he was offered a residency in pathology at a hospital in St. Louis. Almost immediately after moving, however, he received the offer of a lifetime. He had been selected for a coveted surgical fellowship at the Mayo Clinic in Rochester, Minnesota. He leapt at the opportunity.

My brother and I were born in those Rochester years. We were still very small when, one day toward the end of the fellowship, my father turned to my mother and said, "You do know we're never going back to Canada, don't you?"

"Yes," she agreed.

"So, where in the United States would you like to live?" he asked her. "We can move anywhere you want."

"Anywhere but Texas," was her reply.

Of course, you already know that's precisely where we ended up. I can testify that Denton, Texas was a wonderful place to grow up back then, and it's a wonderful place to live and raise a family today.

Now that I'm an adult, a father, and have decades of medical practice behind me, I have a much deeper appreciation for the magnitude of that decision not to go back to Canada. My grandfather had earned a wonderful national reputation there—one my father could have built upon and benefited greatly from. It was home. It was where he had served queen and country. And yet he saw the direction medicine in Canada was heading and ultimately decided that opportunity was more important to him than familiarity.

As far as I know, he never looked back.

He was prescient and way ahead of his time. He foresaw changes coming in Canada that took decades to materialize. Those changes began in 1947 when the province of Saskatchewan established Canada's first provincial hospital insurance program. Ten years later, leaders of Canada's Labour party, operating from socialist assumptions and values, successfully established a national version of that insurance—over the strenuous objections and warnings of doctors, insurance companies, and businesses.

Doctors in Saskatchewan walked out on strike in 1962 when the provincial government there, controlled by the socialist NDP (New Democratic Party) introduced the first public health care program. Doctors knew it would be bad for them and ultimately bad for patients and patient care. But no one listened. The strike collapsed after three weeks.

In 1965, a government commission called for a "universal and comprehensive national health insurance program." A year later, the Canadian parliament created just that—covering 50 percent of health care costs with national taxpayer money and leaving the provinces to cover the other 50 percent with provincial tax collections. By 1977, it was clear to everyone that the system was going broke, so the Labour government scrapped the 50-50 payment system and replaced it with what they call "block funding."

Block funding means that the various categories of health care expenses in Canada are run on a predetermined yearly budget. When a given category's annual budget is depleted, that's it. It doesn't matter where you are in the calendar year, the coffers won't be refilled until the new year comes. This is a tidy way to keep health care costs under control, but it's difficult to respond to people's real medical needs.

Savvy Canadians have learned to pray that if they're going to need serious medical care, that the need will arise in the first half of the year, before the block funding budgets start running dry. You also want to avoid getting sick in January. There is always a rush on medical services right after the first of the year when those budgets are replenished and people who have been waiting for months for a procedure or test can finally see someone.

What Canadians have discovered—and what disappointed Americans will discover if the advocates of universal health care have their way—is that it doesn't matter how great your insurance is if you can't find a doctor to treat you when you're sick. And when you create a system that makes it unrewarding and unpleasant to be a doctor or a nurse, you end up with a shortage of them.

That's an inconvenient truth that produced this 2004 headline above an Associated Press story:

Canadian Doctors Ask Government for $1 billion to Solve Doctor-Nurse Shortage[1]

Apparently money didn't solve the problem because the years 2005 through 2009 brought us headlines such as these in Canada:

Alberta & Saskatchewan Short of Nurses and Doctors[2]
Doctor Shortage Could Jeopardize ER hours at Saugeen Memorial[3]
No Quick Fix for MD Shortage[4]
Shortage Affects Surgeries, Births[5]
Is There a Doctor in the Area?[6]

What options does Canada have in combating this shortage? Really only one. They are doing the same thing the British have been forced to do—they look overseas, often to third world nations. It's a solution fraught with practical and ethical pitfalls, as illuminated by this Vancouver headline from 2007:

Medical Migration: Foreign-trained doctors are helping to staff our health system, but is it ethical to recruit from developing nations?[7]

That's a great question. Is it right to actively recruit the best and brightest from poor nations that desperately need every single trained medical professional they can get? In a 2006 report published in the *Multinational Monitor*, we find:

> Developing countries are facing a critical shortage of health workers because so many of their doctors and nurses are leaving for the green pastures of the rich countries.
>
> Raising the alarm, the World Health Organization says the world is short of 4.3 million medical personnel and this has a "deadly impact" on the countries' ability to fight diseases or respond to new challenges like avian flu.
>
> The migration of doctors and nurses is a "perverse subsidy," says WHO, provided by poor to rich countries. The equivalent of 23 percent of doctors trained in sub-Saharan Africa are working in the rich countries. As many as 37 percent of South African doctors are in rich countries.[8]

Currently in the United States, if there is a nurse shortage it's a market-oriented problem and the market is brilliant at solving it. Salaries, perks, and benefits for nurses rise and more people go into nursing as a career.

But once the government appoints itself as the final arbiter of prices and salaries, a nurse or doctor shortage becomes government problem to be solved by a government bureaucrat or agency. Their track record is not encouraging.

The fact is, we are already in the early stages of a doctor and nurse shortage here as well—in part because the huge baby-boomer demographic group is reaching the age brackets in which medical needs tend to rise. But that's not the only reason.

The late, great radio commentator Paul Harvey once said, "People don't attempt big things for small rewards."

Today, government regulation, exposure to frivolous lawsuits, punishing malpractice insurance premiums, inadequate reimbursements, and crushing paperwork burdens imposed by HMOs and government agencies like Medicare and Medicaid have made entering general practice a deeply unappealing prospect for many of our best and brightest. Getting through medical school is hard and the rewards have been shrinking by the day. It is sobering to contemplate, but an August 2009 survey of doctors revealed that a full 45 percent said they would consider leaving medical practice if the approaches to health care reform being offered at that time were enacted.[9]

Sixty years ago my father left Canada to practice medicine in the United States because the rewards were just beginning to shrink in his native country. A few years ago, my son opted not to follow in the footsteps of three generations of Burgess men. He saw, up close and personal, what his father dealt with week in and week out. He took a look at the rising tide of voices calling for America to follow Canada down the road of socialized medicine. He's a bright young man.

More than a year ago, I mentioned my son's career decision to Newt Gingrich as we were discussing health care issues over coffee at a conference. There he presented me with a question I'd never been asked before. Gingrich said, "If you were to take a pencil and a blank piece of paper, starting from scratch, how would you construct the kind of health care system that you would want to leave for your children and grandchildren?" It was a tough, but important question—one that set me off on a process that has culminated with this book. On the pages that follow, I hope to answer the question: "What kind of system would not only be a rewarding place to practice the healing arts, but just as important, serve patients and family members of patients with excellence."

I am going to draw a clear and compelling picture for you. It is a picture that exposes the deep, systemic problems of the status quo in health care; illuminates the dangers and pitfalls of many of the current "reform" proposals; and points the way to real and lasting improvement in healthcare for all Americans.

I gave up a twenty-five-year medical career to be involved in this debate. What began as a mental, "what if" exercise has now become a lifelong quest for me. My passion and purpose is to articulate and help construct a system in which care is delivered fairly and with excellence to all patients. One that keeps patients—not insurance companies, HMOs, employers, or even doctors—in the driver's seat.

In the remaining chapters, as I share details of my unlikely journey from delivery room to House chamber, I will offer a clear pathway to such a system.

⚕

CHAPTER THREE

EMBRACING THE FAMILY BUSINESS

WHEN I CAME ALONG ON DECEMBER 23, 1950, MY FATHER WAS A SURGEON at the Mayo Clinic in Rochester, Minnesota. My mother says the outside temperature was forty-below-zero on the day of my birth. When my little sister came along two-and-a-half years later, the outside temperature topped out at one hundred five degrees as mother recovered from her delivery in a crowded, un-air-conditioned hospital.

The extreme change in climate conditions was a product of our family having moved nine hundred miles south to Denton, Texas in that intervening gap of time. In the early 1950s, North Texas—much to my mother's dismay—was in the grip of a seven-year spell of heat and drought that reminded long time residents of the brutal Dust Bowl years of a couple of decades earlier. My poor mother had the worst of it—bitter cold and blazing heat.

I was less than a year old when we made that move. As a result, North Texas is the only home I've ever known. Denton in those days was the quintessential small Texas town—a dusty little place filled with good-hearted, hard-working, God-fearing, flag-flying people.

Several events in the 1950s spurred rapid growth in Denton. One of the most unusual came in 1954 when the Federal Civil Defense Administration moved its regional headquarters to Denton from Dallas. Shortly thereafter, construction of a huge underground nuclear fallout bunker was initiated and completed. This Cold War-era complex was the first of several planned sites from which the entire government of the United States could be run in the event of a nuclear war with the Soviet Union. For quite a while it was the only Civil Defense shelter designated as the place from which the President of the United States could direct the country should the unthinkable happen. It seems bizarre and paranoid to younger people today, but kids of my generation remember all too well the duck-and-cover drills and the constant specter of nuclear holocaust.

A few years after our arrival in Denton, a dam construction project overseen by the Army Corps of Engineers created Lake Lewisville, which became the primary water source for Denton. Prior to that, deep artesian wells were the primary source of water for the Burgess family and our neighbors.

It was simply a harsher, more demanding place to live at that time. Or at least it was given the way my father insisted on living. He refused to install air conditioning in our house because he feared too much comfort would make us soft. (Although he did eventually install a window unit in his bedroom, which, due to budget constraints, only ran on the hottest summer nights.)

Dad was determined that we not grow up with any sense of privilege or entitlement simply because our father was a well-respected physician in the community. That determination could lead him to counter-intuitive positions. For example, private schools are sometimes associated with elitism. But Dad sent us to a small private school in the area precisely because he was concerned we might receive too much deferential treatment by teachers and administrators in the public school; or that the kids might be more likely to treat us like we were a big deal.

Perhaps some experiences he had growing up as the son of a prominent doctor in Canada made him especially sensitive to the way doctors and their families could be viewed as special. Of course, you could argue that Dad's goal—which was to simply have us be faces in the crowd—would have been better served by putting us in the much larger public school. At the public school I would have been just one among a graduating class of five hundred. Instead, I graduated in a class of twelve.

Shortly after I was born, the Korean Conflict-era Universal Military Training and Service Act of 1951 lowered the draft age from nineteen to eighteen and a half but provided deferments for college students. By the time I graduated from high school in 1968, the Vietnam War had escalated to the highest level in the history of the long, divisive conflict. And the year before, Lyndon Johnson had pushed through the Military Selective Service Act of 1967. It lowered the draft age to eighteen and raised the upper limit to thirty five. It still granted student deferments, but ended them upon the student's completion of a four-year degree or his twenty fourth birthday, whichever came first.

As a fresh high school graduate, I didn't know much about what I wanted to do with my life. The one thing of which I was certain was that I didn't want to go to medical school. For one thing, given the new draft regulations, I assumed planning to go to med school was pointless. I was going to be entering the military after college no matter what my plans were. My thinking was, "Why work my tail off making good grades for four years if I'm only going to be drafted anyway?" Besides, I viewed military service as an honorable thing. If being drafted was inevitable, then so be it. In my mind, my next stop was Vietnam.

I graduated from High School a year early, when I was seventeen years old. At eighteen I registered for the draft, as was required. What I did not do was request a student deferment. So some time in my sophomore year I received a telegram which began "Greetings." At the appointed time I boarded a bus in Denton and headed down to have my physical.

In the course of the examination, the doctors learned I had suffered from asthma as a kid. After a few more tests, they rendered their verdict. "We don't want you."

Thus I returned to college surrounded by guys who were there specifically because they were concerned about being drafted. They studied like crazy to make sure they stayed in school. I, on the other hand, no longer had that motivation to apply myself. The military didn't want me. As a result, I coasted through another year before I realized I'd better get serious. By that time I had begun to come around to the idea of being a physician.

I knew that if I was to have any hope of getting into medical school, I had better pick a major such as biology and apply myself more diligently to getting my grades up. Adding to my newfound sense of urgency and purpose was watching my older brother wrestle with his post-college plans.

As it turned out, my awakening came a bit too late. Upon getting my bachelors degree in 1972, I decided to stay at the University of North Texas and get a Masters in Physiology.

Finally, in 1974 I was ready to tackle medical school. I applied to several places but had a Plan B in the event I was not accepted by a good school. I would go to Southwestern Medical School and pursue a Ph.D. in biomedical engineering. After sitting on pins and needles through much of the month of June, I finally learned that I had been accepted at the University of Texas Medical School at Houston. I was thrilled, but UTMSH was a three year program at that time. That meant classes started right at the end of June! My wife and I didn't have much time to pack and move.

My wife, Laura, and I had met a year prior when we were both graduate students at The University of North Texas. We married in December, and at the time I was thinking I would not make it to med school. Laura was supportive when there was a dramatic change in plans, but I know the rapid turnaround was unsettling.

As the end of my second year of medical school approached, I faced the decisions with which every prospective doctor wrestles—what specialty to choose and where to apply to do a residency. I had pretty much settled on obstetrics so it was that second question that I had to resolve. I recall a conversation late in that second year in which a fellow student asked, "Where are you thinking about doing your OB residency?" My response was, "Well, I don't know. Maybe Parkland."

I was referring to Parkland Memorial Hospital—a name most people know in association with the Kennedy assassination. It was Parkland to which President John F. Kennedy and Governor John Connelly were rushed after being shot by Lee Harvey Oswald on November 22, 1963. And it was there, in Trauma Room 2, that the President was pronounced dead a short time later. Trauma Room 2 would receive another emergency visitor two days later when Jack Ruby shot Oswald at the nearby Dallas County Courthouse. A few years later, that same emergency room would receive a local prison inmate dying of a pulmonary embolism resulting from lung cancer. His name was Jack Ruby.

Parkland was and is the primary public hospital for Dallas County. When I mentioned my hope of doing my residency there, the enquiring friend's response wasn't exactly encouraging. He laughed out loud and then flatly said, "You could not get into Parkland."

He went on to list all the reasons why that was so. I was in a three-year school. I was one of the last ones admitted. My Med School at the time was on a Pass/Fail system, so we lacked the ranking that other schools employed. He finished with this ringing vote of confidence, "Do you think for a minute that you really have a shot at getting into Parkland?" He walked away chuckling and shaking his head.

His dismissal just doubled my resolve. Undeterred, I talked to somebody on the faculty. They said, "Well, if you want to go to Parkland, what you need to do is go up there early in your senior year and do a month as an extern. That way, you're a known quantity when they are going through the selection process later in the year. Of course, that presupposes you do a great job and they like you."

Taking that advice was no small thing. My wife and I had only weeks earlier welcomed our second baby into our home. She was teaching school to support us and couldn't leave Houston. But we talked it over and decided that being apart for a while was worth the sacrifice.

A short time later, I grabbed a few things and made the five-hour drive up Interstate 45 to Dallas. Bunking in one of the residence halls there, I worked for a month as an acting intern. I was intent on making a good impression in my short time there. As a result, there was no job too small or too nasty for me to take on and do with a song in my heart. I knew this was my only shot at getting a Parkland residency.

Sure enough, later that year I was accepted. Of course, after the residency started, it wasn't long before I started wondering what I'd gotten myself into. Because Parkland is a public hospital, it couldn't refuse to treat any person, regardless of their ability to pay. And as the primary trauma center for the heart of Dallas, we got the worst of the worst of accidents. Those two facts in combination meant we got everything ugly, problematic, messy, or horrific. If no other hospital wanted it, it was thrown at us. In many ways, Parkland was the court of last appeal.

I knew that some of my fellow students were doing cushy, low-stress residencies in suburban private hospitals, and here I was where every day was a new terror. "Why was it, exactly, that I was so all-fired intent on being here?" I murmured out loud from time to time. Of course I knew the answer. It was because that friend had told me I *couldn't* get into Parkland. His derisive dismissal of my chances was like throwing down a gauntlet. It was a personal challenge. A point of pride.

If he hadn't told me Parkland was beyond my reach, I probably wouldn't have even tried for it. Looking back on it now, I'm so glad I did.

One of the things you get from a stint at Parkland is confidence. You may be pretty beat up at the end of it, but you walk out of there feeling there isn't anything you can't handle. By the time I entered private practice as OB/GYN, there was nothing you could throw at me that I hadn't seen. Years later, when a night came along in which I had five back-to-back C-sections, there wasn't a moment in which I thought, "I don't have it in me." I knew I did because those kinds of nights were par for the course at Parkland.

Today residents are limited to eighty-hour workweeks. Not back in my day. The limits came when some started to worry about the toll sleep deprivation and exhaustion were taking on residents' decision making ability. There is wisdom in this, of course. But I must say that the grueling hours I worked helped me know later in life that if I needed to work thirty-six hours straight with no sleep, I could do it and my decisions would be sound. I learned to force myself to make the right decisions, even with a high degree of physical discomfort and fatigue.

That's a powerful piece of knowledge to carry with you into a medical practice. When you get into private practice, there is no one who will show up and say, "Doc, your eighty hours this week are up. I'm here to relieve you." There is no relief. You're it. Once you have obligated yourself to all the responsibilities that launching a private practice entails and, hopefully, your patient load builds, you've just got to do the work that comes in the door. And when your work involves delivering babies, it means being available twenty-four hours a day, seven days a week.

The rigors and demands of training that physicians go through is something that is not well understood by the general public. I know from first hand experience that it is understood even less by the policy makers who wrote the so-called health care reform legislation passed in 2010 over the vigorous objections of doctor-legislators like myself. The preparation to be a doctor is unlike that of almost any other kind of job.

A nephew of mine graduated in 2009 from the medical school at Texas A&M with both an MD and a PhD. This took him seven years beyond the four years he invested in college. But that wasn't the end of his training. He then committed to a seven-year program at the Mayo Clinic in cardiology.

Jay and many others like him weighed heavily on my mind as we debated the Obama-Reid-Pelosi health care proposals throughout the summer of 2009. Here is a guy who is putting fourteen years of his life on the line for this type of training because he wants to be among the absolute best in the world at treating or curing heart disease. He is one of our nation's best and brightest and could pursue any field he wanted. But he chose medicine and is going to be a leading member of the next generation of cardiologists.

Those who ultimately wrote and passed the health care legislation had an obligation to young men and women like Jay. That obligation is one reason I was so offended by the Obama administration's and Speaker Pelosi's repeated demands that we pass a health care reform bill quickly. I remember thinking, "Wait a minute. Wait a minute! This guy and others like him are giving huge chunks of their lives in preparation. Don't we have an obligation to make sure we don't accidentally destroy his ability to help his patients just so you can jam a gigantic bill through Congress before the first of August?" I believe our leaders failed both our doctors and, more importantly, the patients who depend upon them, but that is for a later chapter.

From a technological standpoint, the practice of medicine is a different world today than the world I entered when I started medical school in 1974.

Take breast cancer, for example. Back then, there was no screening per se. Once a woman or her physician discovered a breast lump, she was scheduled for a biopsy. Before that biopsy began, however, the patient signed a consent form for a radical mastectomy. The conventional wisdom at the time was that if you operate and the biopsy reveals that the lump is malignant, you increased the likelihood of dissemination of disease if you didn't proceed immediately to the radical mastectomy.

It made the whole process unbelievably unsettling for women. The statistics said most lumps were benign. Nevertheless, we were asking women to consent to and be prepped for a radical mastectomy before we even knew whether or not there was a malignancy. Women who underwent this process knew to look at the clock as soon as they came out from under anesthesia in the recovery room. "Was I out for thirty minutes or three hours?" A woman's answer to that question told her whether or not a breast had been removed while she was under.

As new technologies and procedures like the lumpectomy with radiation came online, radical mastectomies became less common. Higher resolution imaging techniques came along which enabled us to identify clusters of micro-calcifications on a mammogram long before they would have been perceptible by human touch. Once identified, we could localize that spot with special needles and remove those micro-calcifications. This takes place months or years before any palpable lump is evident.

We have advanced even further in our diagnostic ability recently. It has been a few years since I was in active practice, but I still try to read the journals and keep up. I have noted with optimism a new class of medicines called *aromatase inhibitors*. These compounds stop the production of estrogen in both pre- and post-menopausal women. This results in less estrogen being available to stimulate the growth of a specific type of breast cancer cells. Some encouraging studies have shown aromatase inhibitors to be more effective in treating early-stage, hormone-receptor-positive breast cancer in post-menopausal women than some previous therapies.

My point is, in a few short years, the standard treatment of breast disease has gone from radical surgery to minimal surgery to medical therapy. That is a phenomenal change that has occurred within my professional lifetime. And that is just one small area in the field of medicine. But as I will show in a later chapter, such rapid progress may become a relic of history due to the well-intentioned but terribly misguided "reforms" recently enacted by the government.

It is progress that has made lives better in so many ways. For example, when I started practice, if I recommended a mammogram to someone, it was an intensely emotional, even traumatic event. The patient would go home and tell her husband, "The doctor has scheduled me for a mammogram. He must think I have breast cancer." That was our old world. Now we're in a world in which mammograms are considered routine. In fact, if a doctor doesn't urge a woman over forty to have an annual mammogram, it's considered bad medical practice (although there is some renewed debate about the optimum frequency of mammograms for women with no family history of breast cancer). And once again we encounter interference from a federal agency—this time the United States Public Health Task Force who could dictate practice behavior for both patients and physicians.

Length of hospital stays is another area in which great strides have been made through technology and innovation. When I was doing my residency at Parkland, someone coming in for something as relatively simple as a D and C—dilation and curettage, a procedure that is rarely performed at all any more—meant a night or two in the hospital. In fact, if the patient only spent one night, our quality control officer would be on our backs about why we had discharged so quickly. Thirty years ago we simply avoided one day stays as much as possible. Now we do even hysterectomies as outpatient procedures with minimally invasive surgeries—just a couple of tiny cuts as opposed to a big incision.

The fact is, technology has improved patient care and patient outcomes in essentially every area of medicine. Of course increasingly sophisticated technology has been one of the forces driving health care costs upward. But it is far from the only factor. Many of these cost-increasers are unnecessary and addressable. We'll also explore these in a later chapter.

The Internet has driven another key, technology-related change in the practice of medicine. Not too many years ago, when I told a patient I was concerned that she might have endometriosis, I would explain the condition as best I could and hand her a pamphlet. She would go home, read through the pamphlet, and most likely come back with a dozen questions. Now patients walk into your office telling you they think they have endometriosis because they looked up their symptoms online. Or if they didn't suspect they had the condition, they will go home, Google it, and on their next visit be remarkably conversant in all the treatment options and latest therapies. Of course, there is a down side to this ubiquity of information. The Internet is a vast, unregulated sea of facts mixed with opinions. Not all of the opinions are sound and not all of the "facts" are accurate. Web surfer, beware.

There are some great information resources in the Web, however. Among them are the Mayo Clinic's site, Johns Hopkins' site, and several others. Conversely, there are some truly awful ways to get medical information online. Among the worst is posting a question to a discussion group or message board. Invariably, every person on the board will feel obligated to offer an opinion or a wild guess about your ailment.

The bottom line is, patients today are likely to be sitting in your examining room with their iPhone or Blackberry and looking up their diagnosis before you can get the prescription written. Thus the days of the doctor patting the hand of the patient and saying, "I have all the information you need—just trust me," are over. And on balance, that's a good thing.

We are potentially on the cusp of another revolution in medicine—the complete personalization of diagnosis and treatment. Making this revolution possible is the breakthrough in sequencing the human genome that came a few years ago.

Each one of us is a unique combination of genes passed down to us from our ancestors. Those genetic codes make us more or less likely to develop certain diseases, react to certain drugs, or be susceptible to certain syndromes. It is now possible to have your unique genetic code analyzed. As a matter of fact, I did precisely that recently.

It is not something that should be entered into cavalierly. You're going to find out a lot. And some of it you might prefer not to know.

For me, the news was mixed but the information very helpful. For one thing, I learned I was a very high risk for heart attack. But that is a risk that is very reducible through measures like diet, eating Omega 3 fatty acids such as fish oil, and baby aspirin. I also learned I was at a very low risk for Alzheimer's disease, which was great news. Remembering that low risk does not equal no risk, just like everyone else, I worry when simple facts seem elusive.

A few years ago I went to Microsoft headquarters to give a talk on electronic medical records. While I was there, I met a man who was involved in some of the leading edge genetic testing research. In talking with him I learned that the scans are so specific now that we can detect a genetic predisposition to develop atrial fibrillation. This is a significant breakthrough.

Individuals with atrial fibrillation—something my mother suffered from—will sometimes throw clots from the right side of the heart and have mini strokes or even major strokes.

Back when I did some rotations in the Emergency Room I learned that occasionally someone will come in with all the symptoms of a stroke, and yet are far too young to have had one. The condition then clears and you're left wondering, "Was this a mini stroke in a very young individual or was this just simply a bad migraine with vascular spasm that mimicked a stroke?"

In the course of my conversation with this researcher, he said: "If you can associate a genetic predisposition to atrial fibrillation with that sequence of events, you've identified a group of people that is at high risk for a subsequent stoke and the appropriate preventative steps can be taken. I remember thinking, "Holy cow. It's like pulling the curtain back on the future!" Of course, more study is necessary, but what a powerfully intriguing concept.

There are a growing number of places that offer analyses such as these. Currently a complete scan runs around $2,000 and narrower scans for specific groups of disease, such as cancers or diseases of the heart, are around $500. The costs of such scans will drop rapidly in the future if our wonderful free enterprise system is allowed to do its thing. Competitors to the existing service providers will jump into this exciting, emerging business. Creators of equipment will produce more units at a lower cost. The winner in the end will be the average guy on the street who will get more appropriate, more accurate, more personalized care than ever before. Doctors will be able to focus more on prevention and being proactive—just as I'm doing because I now know of my relatively higher risk of heart disease.

A couple of years ago I was convinced this personalized aspect of medical care was going to be a game changer. But now I'm not as confident. What changed?

One of the tragic ironies of the so-called health care reform legislation passed in 2010 is that it may very well have made such progress far less likely. Just as we were on the verge of making medicine *more* personal than ever before imaginable, the Democratic majority in Congress and President Obama stepped in and forced through something that tends to do just the opposite. Government solutions are *impersonal* by definition. Bureaucracies have an irresistible bias for one-size-fits-all solutions. Ask anyone who regularly needs health care in Canada or the U.K.

It is one of several reasons I fought so hard to stop the worst aspects of the healthcare reform steamroller and offered (in vain) dozens of amendments to improve the parts that couldn't be stopped. I knew that we were right on the exciting edge of developing a new type of medicine. As described by Dr. Elias Zerhouni, the former head of NIH, medicine that was more personal, more predictive, more preventive but requiring more patient participation than ever before. I also knew that the moment America's health care dollars were moved from the hands of patients and into the hands of government bureaucrats applying uniform government-issued standards and quotas, all that promise would be in peril.

The homogenizing, inefficiency-producing, innovation-killing, depersonalizing power of top-down State control can only move us away from the realization of these potentially radical and beneficial changes.

As it turned out, in spite of my best youthful efforts to chart a course different from that of my father and grandfather, I became a doctor. Although there were some maddening moments, the career was rewarding in every way.

The standard career track for people like me is to work hard for as long as possible, invest well, and to retire to the golf course or the lake house. Or perhaps go teach at a medical school where less stress and predictable working hours are the perks. But after almost thirty years of practice, an extraordinary event would put me on a path I couldn't possibly have imagined as a young, sleep-deprived resident at Parkland Memorial.

CHAPTER FOUR

FROM DELIVERING BABIES TO KISSING THEM

I AM A PLANNER BY NATURE. PERHAPS IT COMES WITH THE TERRITORY OF training as a surgeon. Or perhaps people with my particular temperament are naturally attracted to meticulously demanding careers like medicine. In life, I think it is good to always be thinking two or three steps ahead and planning for contingencies. When you are operating on someone, those things are vital.

I suppose that is why I'd been in practice for only a short period of time before I began to wonder what the end of my professional life would look like? Would I reach a point where I would be able to retire? Would I, as many doctors do, simply continue to practice as long as I was physically capable? Sometimes I wondered what I would do if something happened that forced me from the practice of medicine. Who among us doesn't have those daydreams that begin with the supposition, "If I were to do anything else besides what I'm currently doing for a living, what would it be?"

For me and many other doctors, such musings began to take on a little different tone beginning in the early 1980s. I recall the kinds of conversations I had in the surgery lounge, in the coffee room at the clinic, or any area where doctors congregated with a little free time on their hands. My fellow physicians and I were beginning to see some significant changes in the health care system—changes in reimbursement rates, troubling increases in the overall scope and grasp of governmental intervention in medical care with all the attendant regulations, requirements and paperwork. But it wasn't just the rising tide of red tape that troubled us.

Malpractice insurance rates were rising everywhere. Rates jumped in the mid-1970s, continued to rise steadily, and then leapt again in the 1980s. An increasing number of Americans seemed to think catching a doctor in a mistake (real or merely perceived), or sometimes simply experiencing a negative outcome was tantamount to winning the lottery or hitting the jackpot. A new breed of plaintiffs attorneys specializing in suing doctors, hospitals and drug companies started amassing astonishing fortunes by encouraging that very mindset.

Delivering babies was simultaneously stressful and exhilarating—part anxiety and part joy. But the specialty took me away from home and family on many nights. Sometimes, when driving home from the hospital in the wee hours of the morning after delivering a baby, I would find my thoughts wandering down "what if" trails. What if I did something else?

I would invariably remind myself that the practice of medicine is a noble calling. Indeed I sincerely considered it an honor to be a part of a profession whose central calling was to serve the suffering, heal the hurting, and facilitate the entry of new life into the world. Still I could not help but wonder what the future might hold for my practice and me. Sometimes you just never know where life will take you. That, of course, is true for all of us. Events we could not possibly have foreseen end up affecting us in profound ways.

At 8:46 a.m. on the morning of September 11, 2001, I was prepping for what would most likely be a very long surgery. With the patient going under anesthesia, a urologist who would be participating in the surgery and I were scrubbing up when a young nurse burst into the room and said, "Some guy fell off a ladder out in the hall!"

"So is he hurt?" I asked.

"I'm not sure," she said.

"Well, get him down to the Emergency Room," I said. "We're kind of in the middle of something here."

We had a chuckle about the odd interruption and got to the surgery underway. A little later, another nurse burst into the operating room needing to share some news. My fellow surgeon and I looked at each other thinking, "What is it today with people busting in on this procedure? Did someone hang a sign on the door or something?" What began as the revelation that " a plane hit a building" rapidly became much more serious.

Of course, what she shared was sobering. A commercial jet had flown into one of the twin towers of the World Trade Center. We maintained our focus on the long operation at hand, even as additional news reports were fed to us throughout the morning.

"A second jet has hit the other tower. They suspect terrorism."

"The Pentagon is on fire."

"The towers have collapsed."

"A fourth jet has been hijacked. They think it crashed in Pennsylvania."

"All air traffic in the country has been grounded."

By the time the surgery was completed, the news coverage was all about rescue efforts in the rubble pile along with speculation and analysis about who was responsible for the attacks. My poor wife, Laura, watched the events unfold on television alone at home, without the ability to reach me by phone.

The events of that morning obviously changed the lives of many people. Nearly 3,000 innocent lives were snuffed out. Tens of thousands of other Americans lost loved ones or friends. Countless others in New York, Washington, D.C., and elsewhere experienced severe disruptions in their lives.

But, as unlikely as this may seem, in far away and safe North Texas, my life abruptly changed that morning, too. Certainly, like every other American, I was shaken to the core by the events I saw unfold on my television that day. But even as the initial shock dissipated and it became clear

that most things would fairly quickly return to something resembling normal, there was something about the impact of that day that left me feeling
utterly irrelevant in the world.

It almost seemed as if what I did—the practice of obstetrics and gynecology—was totally devoid of any value. I suspect this feeling was rooted in
the fact that my work had nothing to do with protecting my country or my
children's future. In the weeks that followed, my job responsibilities became
more onerous than at any other time in my career. Every day I questioned
my validity, my position in the world, and why it was even important that
I continue to practice.

Instead of finding comfort, or at least some sort of numbness in the
performance of routine tasks, I grew increasingly frustrated by a persistent
feeling of irrelevance. Colleagues or loved ones with whom I shared these
feelings tried to encourage me, reminding me that I was serving mankind
individually in the traditional doctor-patient relationship. Nevertheless, I
felt a guiding, providential hand nudging me toward a larger and definitely
unfamiliar place.

One of the most jarring nudges came about a week after the events in a
late night conversation with a fellow surgeon in the hospital doctor's lounge.

By chance, my friend had been in New York City on September 11. He
got home to North Texas about five days later—having been forced by the
nationwide grounding of all flights to rent a car and drive. He had been
in New York to attend some classes in preparation for his recertification
boards. Not long after his return, we both found ourselves collapsed into
chairs at the doctor's lounge after equally long days. It was my first opportunity to ask him about is 9/11 close encounter.

He said on the morning of September 11, he was sitting in classroom
filled with other surgeons when someone rushed in and interrupted, saying,
"I'm sorry, but we're going to have to cancel this class. There has been a
serious accident. We need everyone to meet downstairs."

There was some understandable confusion and speculation among this
group of doctors about what might have happened. Downstairs in the
lobby of the office they found people huddled around a television set. They

quickly learned about of the commercial jets hitting the main towers of the World Trade Center and processed the reality that our nation was apparently under attack. Before long the face of New York City Mayor Rudy Giuliani appeared on the screen. At the end of his comments he said, "We need anyone in the city with any medical expertise to come downtown."

About that time, someone entered the room and announced that a bus was on the way to transport any doctor who was willing to go to the World Trade Center site and assist. Of course, these doctors were from all over America and few, if any, were licensed to practice in New York. But such technicalities had correctly been tossed aside in the unfolding crisis.

My friend said it was a pretty sobering decision. At that moment it was unclear whether or not additional planes had been hijacked. There were wild rumors circulating of bombs having been planted by terrorist cells. His wife was with him and she intended to stay by his side no matter what. "If you're going to be killed, I want to die with you," she told him. Even more unsettling was a rumor that even Dallas—where they had children living—had been attacked. He tried to anticipate what kinds of injuries he would be treating—surely severe burns, crushed limbs, massive internal injuries, and worse.

When the bus arrived, he took a deep breath and climbed aboard.

As it turned out, they arrived at a makeshift triage center near the World Trade Center complex and braced themselves to receive a wave of severely injured people that never arrived. For the most part, either people got out of the burning buildings relatively unscathed or they died. There was very little in between. But my friend didn't know that when he climbed aboard that bus. As he told me the story, I couldn't help but wonder how I would have responded in that situation.

His story became fuel on a fire that was already burning in my heart and mind. Here my nation was engaged in a life-and-death struggle that political scientist Samuel P. Huntington prophetically called "The Clash of Civilizations."[10-11] Was I just going to keep on delivering babies and going about my business as if nothing had happened? I found myself wrestling with that question repeatedly.

With time these feelings attenuated to a degree, but lingering doubts remained in the back of my mind as to whether or not I was engaged in what I was truly supposed to be doing. Was I on the right path? In quiet moments, that question again rose in my consciousness; challenging the well-ordered world I had meticulously created for myself.

The fact was, I had my life mapped out as a tidy sequence of relatively low-risk, five-year plans that strategically built upon one another until they led to a day that I suspected I would retire. But was this what I was supposed to be doing? Delivering babies, performing surgeries, and managing my practice—lather, rinse, repeat, over and over until retirement? All this while Western Civilization was under assault by a new and lethal breed of fanatic horde?

If not, what was the alternative? What could I do that would be meaningful and contributory? And if I found such a path, would I even have the courage to abandon my secure and familiar existence and embark upon it?

Three months after 9/11, just such a pathway presented itself. Taking this path either required a lot of courage or a healthy measure of good old-fashioned ignorance. Perhaps I had some of both.

On December 13, 2001, the Congressman who had represented the district in which I lived for the past seventeen years announced he would not be seeking reelection. Dick Armey had been the Republican majority leader for almost eight years and was one of the most powerful men in Washington. Now, for the first time in almost two decades, the 26th District congressional seat—considered a "safe seat" for the Republicans—would be open.

The moment I heard the news I sensed this was the challenge my soul had been crying out for. But I wasn't certain. The door stood open before me, but stepping through it was a bracing proposition. In fact, there were moments when I would talk about it that it just sounded crazy as the words were coming out of my mouth. I knew nothing about running a campaign. It took money, time, commitment, and in the end I could just end up making a big fool of myself.

On more than one occasion, I pretty much had myself talked out of making the leap. But each time, the urge and conviction came back stronger than before. Indeed the more I attempted to deny or avoid the decision, the stronger the feeling became that I must offer my name, my experience, and my commitment to the congressional race.

My friends and loved ones' reactions ranged from enthusiastic support to bemused resignation. The nature of the latter response was something along the lines of, "Well, if this is what your mid-life crisis is going to look like, you might as well get on with it and get it out of your system."

A few days after Dick Armey's surprise announcement, I sought the advice of my State Senator, Jane Nelson. I think I was half hoping that she would tell me I was out of my mind, to stop this ridiculous speculation, and to run back to practicing medicine as quickly as possible. Instead, after I told her I was thinking of running for Dick Armey's open seat in Congress, she said, "Oh my gosh, you'd be perfect!" That wasn't the discouragement the reluctant, cautious half of my brain was hoping to hear. Indeed, it seemed that every time I pushed on the door to this crazy path, it opened a little wider.

I suspected I would not be the only one running for the seat on the Republican side and I was correct. Not long after the filing period opened in early January, six candidates had thrown their hats into the ring. As it turned out, one of them was Scott Armey—the son of the retiring Republican Majority leader and presumably the heir to his father's formidable political campaign network of friends and funding. His presence in the race made the rest of us extreme underdogs. Specifically, the odds on *my* long shot effort to make a difference in our nation's capital got a lot longer.

In Texas the party primaries occur early in the year. That meant this doctor who knew virtually nothing about conducting a campaign had to learn and learn quickly. Thus one of my first steps was to hire an experienced campaign consultant. He let me know right away that, given Scott Armey's presence in the race, our goal for the primary election was to come in second and do so without alienating the supporters of the other candidates. If I could accomplish this—and it was by no means an easy task—I would then be in a runoff election with the presumptive frontrunner.

The next step in this strategy would be to woo the vast majority of the voters whose candidate had failed to make the runoff and hope this added up to more than 50 percent of the votes cast in the runoff election. Given the strong Republican majority in the district, the winner of the runoff would almost certainly win the general election on November. This was my theoretical pathway to victory. But it was only a theory. And that pathway involved a steep uphill climb.

My consultant told me the first order of business was raising money because a campaign required a lot of it and no matter how much I raised, the frontrunner was going to have much, much more. The problem was I didn't know the first thing about how to go about it. I simply did the best I could. I also did all the other things candidates are supposed to do—knocking on doors, visiting the barbershops and cafes, and speaking wherever anyone would have me. I found that I genuinely enjoyed meeting the people in the various communities within the district and hearing about their concerns, problems, and hopes. I found that in most cases, they were similar to mine and to those of the patients I'd come to know so well over the years.

Nevertheless, on an almost daily basis something happened that reminded me that I was a political neophyte and very much an outsider to the ways of Washington. One particularly memorable incident came during one of the first candidate debates in which I participated. The moderator asked me what House committees I hoped to sit on if elected.

I had not anticipated being asked that question. As my mind raced to come up with a quick, insightful answer, I quickly realized, to my horror, that I wasn't really sure what committees there were to choose from. I knew about the House Ways and Means committee from Wilbur Mills and Fanny Fox, and the Armed Services committee, but beyond that my knowledge suddenly seemed very thin. What I knew was that my run for the seat was being driven by two primary passions within me. The first was to help strengthen and defend my country against those who wished to do her harm. The other was to bring my understanding of the world of medicine and patient care to Congress in hopes of healing what was ailing our good-but-flawed health care system. I managed to stammer out a vague, semi-coherent response. Fortunately, my opponent's response wasn't much more specific than mine.

Throughout the primary phase of the campaign, I continued to see patients and run my practice as close to normally as possible. Like all rookies, I made other mistakes and missteps throughout the course of the campaign, but none of them proved to be too costly. Before I knew it, the day of primary election voting arrived.

We watched the election returns come in from our living room with a few friends. Our feeling as the votes began to be counted was that I would come in either second or third. Of course there was a huge difference between those two positions. The second place finisher would go on to compete in the runoff with the top vote-getter. Third-place meant all that work and expense was for nothing. The first indicator that things might be going well for that evening was the arrival of a gaggle of reporters and cameras on our doorstep. The early returns were mainly from my home base of Denton County. The reporters indicated that I was in a strong second place and they wanted a reaction from the guy who looked like he would be facing Scott Armey in a runoff. Then the returns from other areas started coming in and my margin began to shrink rapidly and all the reporters departed just as abruptly as they'd arrived.

We were up almost half the night awaiting the final results. Nevertheless, when all the votes were counted, I had a firm grip on second place.

Foolishly, I'd booked a full schedule of appointments for the following day and had to muddle through on limited sleep and wait until evening to get the next phase of the campaign underway. Consistent with our strategy, we courted the voters who had supported the candidates who did not survive the primary. In the end—in a result that surprised virtually all of the experts and ourselves—we won.

Once I emerged as the Republican nominee, those same experts assured me that the hard part was over. Victory in the general election would be a breeze. This time they were right. Thus by April of 2002, the reality finally sank in that by the end of the year, for the first time in more than twenty-five years, I would not be practicing medicine.

The reality meant I had the difficult task of informing my patients about my pending departure from the practice. For some of these families I had been "Doctor B" long enough to have delivered the babies of young women whom I had personally ushered into the world twenty years earlier. I had been an integral part of so many momentous occasions, some considered me an honorary member of the family. And I liked that. I didn't relish the thought of letting my patients know I couldn't serve them any longer. Of course, most of them had followed the election results and made the logical assumptions.

Nevertheless, the ethical and professional guidelines were pretty specific about how this was to be handled. According to the Texas Medical Practice Act, a physician is required to give ninety days' notice prior to terminating their practice. I sent out a letter on June 1 informing my patients that by September 30 my medical duties would be concluded at my clinic. One of the other five partners in my practice would be absorbing my patients, thus no one would lose access to their care.

They just would not be seeing Doctor B anymore. And I needed a coherent letter to tell them this.

The writing of that letter turned out to be a much harder task than I had anticipated. There were so many things I wanted to tell patients in my practice with that letter, but the words were difficult for me to write. In fact the words that I did write seemed absolutely inadequate to express my gratitude for having been able to participate in their medical care for over two decades.

Of course, my patients understood and were largely excited about the new adventure on which I was about to embark. In those final three months of practicing medicine, I was blessed to receive sincere thanks in various forms from essentially a generation of individuals to whom I provided medical care. I do not think until that time I had truly appreciated how much my professional activity meant to the families I had served.

Time and again, a long-time patient would come in for an appointment we both knew would be the last with me. Some were patients who had grown up under my care. Others had simply grown older with me. In every case, I was grateful for the pictures or stories they shared with me about our relationships over the years. Some remembrances were of joyous occasions like an uneventful delivery. Others were of a shared sorrow. Many of the most poignant and gratifying were recollections of a health-related crisis in which I had been able to make a difference for the better.

I suddenly gained a fresh appreciation of, and gratitude for, the confidence my patients had expressed in me over the years—confidence they demonstrated by referring the dearest friends and loved ones into my care. As a result, my practice had grown and thrived, even though I came into medicine at a time in which advertising and marketing for doctors didn't exist. In fact, it was frowned upon. "Good doctors don't have to advertise," we were told. And I didn't. My patient base was built upon classic referral patterns—word-of-mouth recommendations from other patients.

To *make a difference*. It's all any of us really want to do. But I guess when you're in the midst of it, consumed with all of the distractions and pressures of the moment, it is easy to completely overlook the blessings that are right in front of your face. In the closing weeks of my medical practice, I discovered I'd failed to notice some of the most important things. A look of gratitude; the acknowledgement of a little bit of extra effort expended; the relief in a young mother's voice because you've spent a little additional time at the end of a very long day.

After a couple of weeks of these daily outpourings of appreciation and affirmation, I started wondering if maybe I'd made a mistake! I had known all along that I would miss those exciting moments with brand new parents in the delivery room. I also knew I would miss the adrenaline rush that comes with the performance of a successful surgery. What I hadn't anticipated was the low-key, but very humanly gratifying times of client interaction in the treatment room. The events of September 11 had left me feeling as if what I was doing didn't matter. Now, in the midst of this outpouring of appreciation and affirmation, I got a profound and humbling sense that what I had been doing mattered very much.

Looking back on this departure now nearly ten years later, I find I miss the practice of medicine much more than I could have ever anticipated. To be honest with you, hardly a night goes by that I don't dream about some aspect of the practice of medicine. Generally these dreams involve some sort of conflict about needing to be in two places at one time for my patients. I'm sure an armchair psychologist could draw some interesting conclusions about what my subconscious mind is trying to process through these recurring dreams. But whatever it is, one thing is crystal clear: A decade after I saw my last patient, medicine is still very much on my mind and in my heart.

In a very real, very significant way, I feel as if I'm still working to make a difference for my patients. Yes, I made my decision to run for Congress while the debris pile of twisted steel, pulverized concrete, and shattered lives was still smoldering at Ground Zero. I made it with a compelling need to feel as if I was doing what I could to help our country in a time or war. But I also knew that if God, in very improbable circumstances, had somehow made a way for a doctor like me to go to Washington, then surely my first-hand understanding of what was wrong (and right) with our system of health care wasn't going to go to waste.

Of course, at that moment in history, Republicans held majorities in both houses of Congress. And a new, young Republican president was in the White House and most of the nation had rallied to him in this atmosphere of crisis. It seemed to me that the possibilities of getting some positive, helpful changes and adjustments to the American health care system were bright—the kind of changes I will lay out in a later chapter.

As I began looking for an affordable place for my wife and I to rest our heads in Washington—no small feat, by the way—I could not possibly have imagined that in a couple of short election cycles, an unpopular war and a host of other factors would have sent that president's approval ratings plummeting to record lows. Or that my fellow Republicans failure to live up to our own principles regarding the growth and expense of government might cost us or majorities in both houses of Congress.

The fact is, I had scarcely gotten fully oriented and acclimated to the ways of getting things done in our nation's capital before I found myself fighting proposals that would make our health care system much worse rather then leading the charge for making it better.

I will chronicle in detail the struggle over what came to be called the 2010 Patient Protection and Affordable Care Act in a later chapter. For now it is only important to note that even though the measure passed, there was an intense battle for the soul of what has been the greatest system of health care innovation and delivery the world has ever seen. Imperfect? Yes. Improvable? Without a doubt. But all of that is now in grave danger if we fail to undo much of what was done hastily, foolishly, and largely behind closed doors. Vast changes have been set in place by people in Congress and by a White House that doesn't know the first thing about how the health care systems works in this country. Heroic efforts may be necessary to prevent some disastrous outcomes in the months and years to come. As I write, some of those negative effects are already manifesting. That means that a unique opportunity to help more people than I'd ever imagined possible lies before me.

I obviously cannot predict the future. I only know that I must be prepared. There will be no consolation prize. There, will be no second place. This is a contest that simply must be won. True victory will mean the preservation of some component of free enterprise within the practice of medicine, and not forsaking the concept of individual liberty and self-determination on the part of the patient.

To be sure, the complexities involved in paying for health care are significant. There may yet be some significant compromises that have to be struck. Simply giving up and giving in to the wishes of the other side—statists with no regard for the power of the free enterprise system and little understanding of the immutable laws of market forces—is not an option.

I ran for Congress and remain there for healthy people, not for healthy statistics.

Of course, all of this lay in the future and beyond my foresight as a newcomer in Congress. The labyrinthine ways, customs, and process of Washington were all new to me. I am wired like a doctor. The steps to curing an illness are simple and threefold: examine, diagnose, and treat.

As I was about to find out, things are rarely that simple in Washington, D.C.

CHAPTER FIVE

D.C. THROUGH A DOCTOR'S EYES

In the heart of Washington, D.C., the House and Senate office buildings are connected to the Capitol complex by tunnels under the streets. These subterranean passageways allow members of Congress to get from their offices in the Cannon or Rayburn buildings to the Capitol's legislative chambers without having to go outside. Many members prefer to use them because they not only provide shelter from the weather extremes the nation's capital is prone to experience, but also because the tunnels allow them to avoid reporters, protestors, crackpots, wanna-be You Tube heroes with pocket video cameras, and other hazards of the job. But from my first days in Washington, I have shunned the tunnels unless a downpour of rain was in progress.

I like the visual reminder that the majestic Capitol dome provides. I have found that if I just descend into the bowels of a busy office building and then emerge in a hallway outside the House Chamber, it is too easy to think of what we're doing as theoretical, technical, and soulless. Walking out of the Cannon office building and onto the sidewalk fronting Independence

Avenue, you see that gleaming white dome soaring high in the sky right before you with the bronze figure of Freedom crowning it. It's an awe-inspiring sight. And it never fails to remind me that what I'm about to do has huge implications in the lives of people back home and in neighborhoods like it all over America.

I arrived in Washington, D.C. in early November 2002 for the two-week orientation that precedes the beginning of every new Congress. For a God-and-Country Texan like myself, it was a heady and surreal experience. On one of our first nights there, for example, Laura and I attended a traditional candlelight dinner in the Capitol Building's "Statuary Hall." with larger-than-life statues of American legends like Ethan Allen, Daniel Webster, William Jennings Bryan, and fellow Texan Stephen F. Austin looking on. There was a reception for incoming freshmen and their spouses at the Library of Congress, hosted by Speaker of the House Dennis Hastert and new Senate Majority Leader Bill Frist. Here I was, a country doctor, sitting in the same building so steeped in history and listening to newsmakers speak.

It was a lot to take in. But I think the most impacting moment of all came one of the first times I simply headed up a marble stairway toward the House Chamber. As I climbed the stairway, I couldn't help but notice how worn the marble was in the central part of each step. In that moment I realized I was looking at the erosion and weathering of more than 200 years worth of footfalls. And then I thought about all the history those stair-climbers witnessed and made. The hair on the back of my neck stood up as I realized I was placing my foot in the same spot trod by many of the towering figures who captured my imagination as a boy growing up in Texas such as Davy Crockett and Sam Houston. I thought about the historic votes that had been taken in the House Chamber—declarations of war, advancements in civil rights, articles of impeachment—and how the people who had shouldered the responsibility of casting those votes walked this way before and after the moment of decision.

That initial two weeks of orientation was a blur of learning. But not every educational moment was an inspiring one. A few served as stark reminders that Washington is a place of partisan guerrilla warfare and raw ambition. For example, toward the end of that orientation period came the time for the big bipartisan group photo of incoming freshmen of the 108th Congress. We lined up on the east steps of the Capitol and I somehow managed to be placed on the first row. "This is cool," I thought to myself. But no sooner had gotten settled in my spot when an intense, wiry man approached me and said, "I'm going to need you to move. This gentleman needs to be in this spot." I had no idea who was speaking to me, but I obediently found another spot in one of the rows farther back.

A little later I discovered the name of the person who moved me from my prime spot. It was a fellow freshman Congressman from the Chicago area named Rahm Emanuel. He had wanted to see one of his colleagues on the front row of the photo because he considered him a rising star in his party, so he took it upon himself to make a place for him. Emanuel's zeal for promoting his fellow Democrats would not go unnoticed or unexploited by his party. A few years later he would be named Democratic Congressional Campaign Committee chairman and in that post become the architect of the Democrats' 2006 takeover of the House that put Nancy Pelosi in the Speaker's chair. And in 2008 he would be named newly elected President Barack Obama's White House Chief of Staff. From that post, he would be instrumental in guiding the Democrat's ambitious remaking of America's health care system in a more European image—working with Speaker Pelosi to twist the arms and cut the deals necessary to ensure its passage at any cost. Thus it is no exaggeration to say that few individuals in America bear more responsibility than Emanuel for the deeply flawed, profoundly misguided mess that resulted.

Of course, the health care system that existed before Rahm Emanuel helped President Obama and Nancy Pelosi ram through that 400,000-word leviathan of a bill was far from perfect. Indeed the promise of improving the quality and affordability of health care for all Americans was one of the key reasons I came to believe that Congress could use another physician in its ranks.

As I mentioned in the previous chapter, I had been caught off guard during my first campaign by a question about which committees I hoped to get on if elected. After my narrow escape in that debate, I did my homework about the House committee system. I was determined to have a meaningful answer ready should that question arise again.

What my research revealed surprised me. Given my long experience as physician, I started looking for the committee that would address health care issues. After all, the health care industry now represents about one-sixth of our entire economy and, as the baby boomer population continues to age, that percentage can only increase. A quick scan of the list of committees and subcommittees failed to turn up anything called "Health Care." To my surprise and disappointment, I learned there was no committee assigned to health care issues. Instead, I learned that the jurisdiction for health care actually resides within three separate committees. The Committee on Energy and Commerce, the Committee on Ways And Means, and the Committee on Education and Workforce, all shared responsibility for some component of health care policy.

I remember thinking at the time that perhaps this was for the best. If there were a single congressional entity for health policy, it might be too powerful. It also occurred to me that the framers of the Constitution did not build any infrastructure for health care matters into our system of government because they viewed them as personal matters rather than concerns of the government. The Founding Fathers likely saw no role for the federal government in the very private, very personal relationship between a patient and his or her doctor.

Nevertheless, I had run for Congress to make a difference—both for the people of my district and for my country. Yet those "big three" committees were off limits to freshmen. I discovered that it took some significant seniority to get a seat on those bodies that were going to be dealing with health care matters, and that getting a desired assignment to a congressional committee involved a political process in and of itself. This was a little bit difficult for me to accept. I had just come through a full year of very intense campaigning, now only to find that it was necessary to engage in another type of campaign just so I could get a seat on a committee that made sense for me and for my constituents. It was also somewhat of a surprise to learn that most of the other members of my freshman class were already engaged in the campaign for committee assignments—that indeed some had been involved in a committee campaign prior to their election.

Given that any committee that contained a health-care jurisdiction was off limits to me as a freshman, I had to quickly decide what other options made sense for me and for those I had been sent to Washington to represent. As it happens, a confluence of major highways, railways and airports run through or are very near my district. Of all the committee positions that were available to a new congressman, a seat on the transportation committee seemed to provide the most value for my constituents. Knowing that I was already behind the curve, I immediately embarked on a campaign for a seat on the Committee on Transportation & Infrastructure.

The process surrounding the handing out of committee assignments is highly charged and intensely competitive. Considerations such as the state in which a member resides, the difficulty he or she might face during reelection, and other less tangible factors were considered when handing out committee assignments. Fortunately, I was able to successfully argue for a seat on the Transportation Committee.

Jockeying for committee assignments wasn't the only process that involved heavy politicking. Right in the middle of that dizzying two-week interval for orientation, we all had to vote in our respective party's leadership elections. The Republicans held majorities on both houses of Congress when I was elected. That meant we would be voting on who would be Speaker of the House, Majority Leader, Majority Whip, Majority Caucus Chair, and so forth.

Of course, many of us incoming congressmen, particularly those of us who had not been deeply involved in the machinery of politics in the past, were not well positioned to cast an informed vote on who should hold these positions. And in the years to follow, I would come to appreciate just how important these decisions are. In the first few days in D.C. you are voting for the leaders that will provide the direction, strategy, and tone for much of the work you will do in Congress. They will also serve in large measure as the "face" of the party to the broader public. Thus we freshmen were asked to participate in crucial decisions with minimal information.

This becomes especially important when there is a large incoming freshman class and the newcomers make up a big percentage of the total vote. This importance is compounded when the election produces a change from minority to majority party status, as has been the case twice over the last twenty years. Such a shift means much more control of the congressional agenda will be in the hands of these party leaders.

Still another task facing a brand new member of Congress is hiring staff for both the Washington and district offices. This exercise is the equivalent of launching a multi-state business in at least two locations on a fixed budget, on a short timeline, and with the opportunity for spectacular failure ever at hand. For help in staffing the Washington office we were directed to a desk in the basement of the Rayburn building. Upon it lay thousands of applications from job seekers. But how to choose? Should I be interviewing individuals with political experience? Or is it better to select people with policy expertise instead? Are applicants with advanced or professional degrees to be preferred? Or should I simply favor Texas residents? It is difficult to make wise selections when you're really not sure what it is you need.

Fortunately, I began the process by recalling some advice my mother offered many years ago when I was first setting up a medical practice. She told me the most important person in an office is the individual who answers the phone. I learned that she was absolutely correct. The receptionist provides the initial contact with the patient (or constituent), and sets the tone for his or her entire experience. I quickly determined that the person who answered the phone in each of my offices must be pleasant, knowledgeable, service-oriented, and have a passable Texas accent.

In this critical hiring phase, I found I had another advantage. As I was moving in and setting up shop, longtime Texas senator Phil Gramm was retiring and moving out. That meant many of his experienced staff members were out of a job and searching for new openings. I was able to make a number of good selections from this attractive applicant pool—they knew Capitol Hill and they knew Texans' values and concerns. Of course John

Cornyn, the incoming senator taking Gramm's seat, was interested in talking to these job seekers, too. But I had quickly jumped on the opportunity to hire some key Gramm staffers. Senator Cornyn good-naturedly gave me the nickname, "the rustler," because I had been so effective in rounding up key talent from his predecessor.

The next jolt to this newcomer was learning that I needed to hire a press person. "Are you kidding me?" I remember saying. "I need a Press Secretary? Me, a simple country doctor needs a press secretary?" As it turned out, I did. Both in Washington and in the district it is not enough to simply do a good job for your constituents. If you don't consistently communicate what you are doing, their perception can quickly get out of line with reality. It also became evident that communication *effort* does not always mean communication *success*. That reality makes a Communication Director one of the most critical members of the congressional staff.

Following this hectic period of moving, hiring, acclimating, and learning, I eventually settled into the rhythms and routines of life in the House. In those initial years health care issues were not on the front burner in most policymakers minds. The post-9/11 issues surrounding the global war on terrorism, along with the two wars being waged in Iraq and Afghanistan, dominated the headlines and occupied the lion's share of our deliberative attention.

Nevertheless, there were some opportunities in my first term to weigh in on medical issues. We wrestled with the heartbreaking and gut-wrenching Terri Schiavo case. And we voted to extend the ban on federal funding embryo-destroying stem cell research.

Please note the terms "federal funding" and "embryo-destroying" in the previous sentence. Opponents of this ban and their allies in the news media invariably wrote or spoke of "Bush's ban on stem cell research" or described the legislation we passed as a "ban on stem cell research." Both characterizations are false and misleading. A majority of us in Congress agreed with President Bush that taxpayer dollars should not be allocated for a practice as ethically controversial as destroying embryos to harvest stem cells. Researchers, however, have always been free to conduct such research with private sector funds and indeed they have. Furthermore, federal money continued to flow to fund other promising avenues of stem cell research. The claim that we "banned stem cell research" is simply not true.

Here it is probably useful to mention some of the Republican accomplishments of the decade preceding this healthcare vote. During the Obamacare debate one of the criticisms that was fired at Republicans, in addition to that of having no ideas, was that we had ten years to fix the problems and had simply failed to address them. While it is not the purpose of this discussion to go into those areas of previously enacted policy in detail, I do feel compelled to mention the State Children's Health Insurance Program which was passed in 1996, welfare reform which was passed in 1996, and expansion of health savings accounts and prescription drug coverage for seniors, which passed in the Medicare modernization act of 2003. While there has been some criticism of the Part D prescription drug benefit for seniors, I feel it is worthwhile to mention that this was the number one healthcare issue when I ran for office in 2002. There were continued calls to expand the entitlement side of Medicare to include this benefit. The program as enacted more closely resembles prescription insurance than it does an expansion of an entitlement, and does contain several market principles in order to hold down costs. It can be argued that the four dollar generic prescriptions now available at various retail pharmacies are a direct result of price transparency and efforts to hold down costs that were incorporated in the Medicare modernization act.

At one point during my first year in the House, Michigan Congressman John Dingell, Jr. introduced a bill that would create a national health insurance system along the lines of Britain's socialized National Health Service. This was far from the first time Dingell, whose district lies in western Detroit and its suburbs, had introduced such a bill. (Nor would it be the last.) In fact, he had been introducing it in every session of Congress since he took over his father's seat in 1955. But the legacy of Dingell's push to create a new universal entitlement of health care extends back further still. Dingell had taken over his seat from his father, John Dingell, Sr. He, too, was a New Deal Democratic Congressman and champion of a New Deal–style national health-care system. He introduced his first bill along these lines in 1943, and did so every year until his death. When Dingell took over the seat from his father, the older man's bill was under consideration but never voted on. Thus, the son's annual introduction of a similar bill right up to and including my first year in Congress and continuing until, at the age of eighty-three, he finally saw his father's New Deal dream become a reality.

With the passage of the so-called Patient Protection and Affordable Care Act of 2010, the government took the first big step toward nationalizing the health care industry and thereby making every American a virtual ward of the State. As a matter of fact, once the national government is footing all or a significant part of the bill for everyone's health care, it means there is no area of our personal lives that will not directly or indirectly be the business of the government—from what you eat, to how much you weigh, to how much television you watch. Any activity that has a potentially negative impact on your health will arguably be the concern of the government bureaucrats assigned to "manage" health care costs.

That is not hyperbole or speculation. We need only look to the U.K., which has had a single-payer system in place for decades. There, the fact that the taxpayers are footing the bill for everyone's health care provides the justification for inserting the nose of government into every aspect of British life. But as a 2010 article in the British newspaper *The Telegraph* reported, such efforts are wildly expensive and simply don't work:

> More than £350 million [$550 million] of taxpayers' money was spent by the Labour government on health campaigns urging the public to drink and eat less, exercise more and practice safe sex, it can be revealed today.
>
> Spending on the poster, television and cinema campaigns rose 30 fold during Labour's time in power, yet failed to prevent the growth of the "lifestyle" diseases the money was meant to combat. Over the same period, the number of sexually transmitted infections doubled, while levels of obesity and binge drinking soared.[12]

This is the inevitable result of shifting responsibility for health care from individuals and families to bureaucrats looking at spreadsheets.

To be fair, the health care bill that finally passed in November of 2009 did not put in place the "single-payer," universal, government-run system that Dingell and his perennial legislative ally, the late Ted Kennedy, had long wanted. But it was a huge step in that direction and, unless reversed, will inevitably lead to one, as I will discuss in a later chapter. As a matter of fact, with polls continuing to show that government-run health care is more unpopular than ever, proponents of socialized medicine who were actually disappointed that the bill didn't go far enough toward a single payer system have now cleverly changed their terminology. Now that the public is savvy to terms like *single payer system*, they're talking instead about "Medicare for all." It's a different name for the same concept. As you may know, the current Medicare program is a government-subsidized insurance program for Americans over sixty-five, and all of the current projections indicate that it will bankrupt our country not too many years from now unless significant, painful changes are made. So, believing that "Medicare for all" will do anything but make that situation far worse, far faster and involves a type of math with which I am not familiar.

Of course, all of these debates lay years in the future during my first term in the House. And in the years that followed, Dingell's bill continued to die in committee each time it was revived—just as it had in the previous six-plus decades he and his father had been offering it.

It seemed to me that, with a majority of Americans firmly opposed to socialized medicine, the long-cherished progressive dream of institution-alizing cradle-to-grave care for every American (whether they wanted it or not) remained unlikely to ever be realized as long as Republicans held control of one of the houses of Congress or the White House. Even after the Democrats took control of both the House and the Senate in 2006, I still believed that the American people's well-founded skepticism about government-driven solutions would keep my colleagues across the aisle from trying anything too bold or sweeping.

Then the fall of 2008 came and with it the confluence of a presidential election featuring the most liberal Democratic candidate since George McGovern; a severe economic recession; and a worldwide crisis in capital markets. It was a blend of extraordinary events that emboldened some to think about what had previously been unthinkable—a government takeover of an industry representing one-sixth of the entire U.S. economy.

CHAPTER SIX

NEVER LET
A GOOD CRISIS
GO TO WASTE

IT WAS A LITTLE SURREAL. IT WAS SEPTEMBER 17, 2008, AND I WAS SIT-
TING IN a wood-paneled, red-carpeted, velvet-curtained committee meeting room listening to my colleagues on the Health subcommittee of The
Committee of Energy and Commerce hold forth about America's uninsured. The figure "47 million uninsured individuals" was being thrown
around liberally and repeatedly.

In his opening remarks, the committee chairman, Frank Pallone
(D-New Jersey), described the current state of health care in America as "a
crisis." In fact, he said, "When it comes to our nation's health care system, I
think there is at least one thing we can all agree on. That is, our health care
system is in crisis." I remember thinking at the time, "I guess it depends
upon your definition of *crisis*."

I had that thought, and describe the proceedings as surreal, because
outside our chamber doors that day, a genuine crisis was unfolding, the
kind of potentially devastating series of events for which the overused and
oft-abused term *crisis* at one time be reserved. To be specific, the global

system of credit and finance on which the world's modern economies depend was tottering on the brink of collapse. And here we were speechifying and posturing about who was covered by what kind of insurance.

Two days earlier, Bank of America, with some prodding from the Federal Reserve, agreed to acquire the financially ailing Merrill Lynch for about $50 billion, in a deal merging one of the nation's biggest banks with one of its biggest and oldest brokerage firms. The very same day the venerable old giant of Wall Street, Lehman Brothers, filed for bankruptcy protection after negotiations fell through to have Bank of America buy that company as well.

A few days prior to that, Treasury Secretary Henry Paulson had announced the emergency takeover of Fannie Mae and Freddie Mac, essentially placing the government in charge of the two mortgage giants that own or back more than $5 trillion in American mortgages. The Treasury Department simultaneously agreed to provide up to $200 billion in loans to the cash-starved firms that were the vital sources of mortgage funding for banks and other home lenders.

Global anxiety about the financial markets had been building all week, but it was the Lehman bankruptcy that really tipped the bucket of panic over. As one British newspaper described it:

> The reality of [Lehman's] collapse stunned markets and delivered a paralyzing shock to the financial system. Terrified banks would barely lend to each other for more than 24 hours in what Bank of England Governor Mervyn King described as the worst crisis since the First World War. Every day that followed brought a new seismic event.
>
> On the Tuesday that week, US insurer AIG was given a taxpayer bailout, Wednesday saw a takeover of UK's Halifax Bank of Scotland by Lloyds TSB - with competition rules waived in the interests of keeping HBoS from collapse and nationalisation. [13]

It was ugly and getting uglier by the hour. Secretary Paulson was scheduled to come address the Republican conference in the United States House of Representatives, but canceled at the last minute because of "other obligations." I didn't perceive that to be a good sign. This was a Thursday and the Democratic leadership of the House of Representatives canceled Friday's votes and adjourned later that afternoon.

But there I was trapped in that hearing room. The health subcommittee hearing continued well into the afternoon beyond the time the House had officially adjourned for the weekend. Looking back on this now, it seems almost bizarre that this discussion of paying for health insurance for "47 million" people should continue while an economic tsunami was potentially bearing down on every family in America and on families around the world.

By the way, about that 47 million uninsured Americans. That's a number that would continue to be tossed out unendingly by advocates of a bigger government role in health care. There was just one problem with that figure. It was deeply misleading.

Here are some additional insights into the claim of 47 million uninsured courtesy of the non-partisan Annenberg Public Policy Center's FactCheck.org. They said:

We find that many of the numbers cited are accurate, but may need to be seen in context to get a true picture.

- The Census Bureau estimates that 45.7 million lacked health insurance at any given time in 2007. But fewer lacked coverage for the full year, and more did without for one or more months during the year. All three numbers are likely to be higher for 2008 due to massive job losses.
- Twenty-six percent of the uninsured are eligible for some form of public coverage but do not make use of it, according to The National Institute for Health Care Management Foundation. This is sometimes, but not always, a matter of choice.
- Twenty-one percent of the uninsured are immigrants, according to the Kaiser Family Foundation. But that figure includes both those

who are here legally and those who are not. The number of illegal immigrants who are included in the official statistics is unknown.

- Twenty percent of the uninsured have family incomes of greater than $75,000 per year, according to the Census Bureau. But this does not necessarily mean they have access to insurance. Even higher-income jobs don't always offer employer-sponsored insurance, and not everyone who wants private insurance is able to get it.

- Forty percent of the uninsured are young, according to KFF. But speculation that they pass up insurance because of their good health is unjustified. KFF reports that many young people lack insurance because it's not available to them, and people who turn down available insurance tend to be in worse health, not better, according to the Institute of Medicine.[14]

As you can see, a significant percentage of that oft-cited 47 million folks were not uninsured for the entire year; could obtain insurance if they wanted it; or were illegal aliens who arguably should not have health coverage at the expense of U.S. taxpayers.

Nevertheless, witnesses in committee continued to provide testimony, and my fellow members on the committee continued to ask questions. As a preview into how difficult paying for health care for the uninsured was going to be, estimates provided to the committee that day varied from $60 billion to $800 billion annually. And to provide a note of context, within fourteen days Congress would approve a one-time financial "bailout" package whose cost exceeded $800 billion.

At the time I was a health-care advisor and spokesman for the John McCain campaign. When the hearing finally adjourned that afternoon, I caught a plane for Orlando, Florida to provide Senator McCain's perspective on health care reform to a forum put on by the *Washington Post* writers' group. I gamely traveled to the appointed spot and gave the standard McCain health care stump speech and answered questions from the audience, all the while wondering what the future held for us with this gathering financial storm.

There was one thing of which I was certain. This storm didn't bode well for the McCain campaign. It was hard to believe that just a few short weeks earlier, Senator McCain had selected Sarah Palin as his running mate and immediately surged to a slim but encouraging lead in the polls for the presidential horse race. Those of us on the campaign had a few heady days to contemplate what the country would be like under a McCain presidency, before it was all washed away in a tidal wave of economic bad news.

McCain's nomination had been based, in part, on the belief that this was a "national security" election—that the thing foremost on the minds of mainstream Americans was winning the global war on terrorism, keeping American families protected from another Al Qaeda attack, and victory in the two wars underway in Iraq and Afghanistan. But suddenly the race became an "economy" election—an issue which McCain, though an honorable and patriotic man, wasn't ideally suited to inspire confidence. Defense was the seasoned navy airman's strong suit.

As the global financial crisis swelled, the Republican and Democratic nominees for president, both sitting senators, had to return to Washington DC to vote on the bailout package—officially called, "The Emergency Economic Stabilization Act of 2008." Nevertheless, it was Senator McCain who bore the brunt of the country's anxiety. After all, it was a Republican president in the White House, and Mr. McCain was the Republican nominee. Never mind that both senators voted in favor of the bailout, it was Senator McCain that a majority of swing voters seemed to hold responsible.

This extraordinary sequence of events left Senator McCain badly damaged politically and, conversely, Senator Barack Obama in a favorable position as the initial momentum provided by the Palin nomination was swamped by wave after wave of economic bad news.

Just prior to that vote on the first bailout package, Congress was held in town by a procedural maneuver colloquially known as "martial law." This provision, enacted by the Speaker of the House, means that a major provision may be brought up for a vote in as little as one hour's time and that every member of Congress must stay literally at their desk, by the phone, awaiting action on the bill. Unfortunately for us it took a full eight days for that bill to come to the floor of the House. And all during that time I could do little but watch the unfolding drama on the cable television stations as the McCain campaign took on more and more water.

Afterward, I continued my work as a surrogate spokesman on health care for the McCain campaign through the month of October, continuing to hope and believe that the effort could accomplish what now seemed impossible— that is, push through to victory in the face of fierce economic headwinds.

To be honest, it was difficult to fight back a gathering sense of gloom and apprehension about the impending outcome and what it might mean for the country. Based on what I had seen in my handful of years in Washington I feared that, should the voters put the man who was demonstrably the most liberal member of the U.S. Senate into the White House while simultaneously giving Speaker Pelosi and Senate Majority Leader Reid stronger majorities in their respective houses of Congress, the country would be moved in precisely the wrong direction and at a very critical time for our nation. As it turned out, the reality proved much worse than my grimmest fears.

Nevertheless, I soldiered on and that meant not only learning the finer points of Senator McCain's health care plan, but also studying and understanding what Mr. Obama was proposing as well. Indeed, in seventeen debates across various locations in the country I heard Senator Obama's surrogates talk about his vision for health care reform.

As it turned out, what the future president's surrogates outlined during the campaign bore little resemblance to what the Democrats eventually passed, the President signed, and is now universally known as "Obamacare." For example, the campaign 2008 version of Senator Obama's health care proposals did not include mandates, except for children, and for every American who lacked health insurance, it provided a standard PPO type plan in the Federal Employees Health Benefits Plan. Ironically this is where the figure of $800 billion a year originated from during our health subcommittee hearing.

As a matter of fact, during the Democratic primaries, Senators Obama and Clinton clashed repeatedly over the issue of health insurance mandates (provision that would require every American to have a certain level of health insurance coverage whether they wanted it or not.) Hillary Clinton frequently criticized Mr. Obama's health care approach precisely because it did not contain a mandate provision. Obama roundly blasted Senator Clinton because her proposal *did* include mandates. During their primary debate in Austin, Texas on February 21, the two candidates had a lively exchange about health care mandates. What follows is a portion from the debate transcript:

> **Senator Obama:** So we've got a lot of similarities in our plan. We've got a philosophical difference, which we've debated repeatedly, and that is that Senator Clinton believes the only way to achieve universal health care is to force everybody to purchase it.
>
> And my belief is, the reason that people don't have it is not because they don't want it but because they can't afford it.
>
> And so I emphasize reducing costs.
>
> (APPLAUSE)
>
> And as has been noted by many observers, including Bill Clinton's former secretary of labor, my plan does more than anybody to reduce costs, and there is nobody out there who wants health insurance who can't have it.
>
> Now, there are legitimate arguments for why Senator Clinton and others have called for a mandate, and I'm happy to have that debate.
>
> **Senator Clinton:** This is a significant difference. You know, Senator Obama has said it's a philosophical difference. I think it's a substantive difference.
>
> He has a mandate for parents to be sure to ensure their children. I agree with that. I just know that if we don't go and require everyone to have health insurance, the health insurance industry will still game the system. Every one of us with insurance will pay

the hidden tax of approximately $900 a year to make up for the lack of insurance.

And you know, in one of our earlier debates, John Edwards made a great point. It would be as though Social Security were voluntary. Medicare, one of the great accomplishments of President Johnson, was voluntary.

(APPLAUSE)

I do not believe that is going to work. So it's not just a philosophical difference. You look at what will work and what will not work. If you do not have a plan that starts out attempting to achieve universal health care, you will be nibbled to death, and we will be back here with more and more people uninsured and rising costs.

Senator Obama: Number one, understand that when Senator Clinton says a mandate, it's not a mandate on government to provide health insurance, it's a mandate on individuals to purchase it. And Senator Clinton is right; we have to find out what works.

Now, Massachusetts has a mandate right now. They have exempted 20 percent of the uninsured because they have concluded that that 20 percent can't afford it. In some cases, there are people who are paying fines and still can't afford it, so now they're worse off than they were. They don't have health insurance and they're paying a fine.

(APPLAUSE)

In order for you to force people to get health insurance, you've got to have a very harsh penalty, and Senator Clinton has said that we won't go after their wages. Now, this is a substantive difference. But understand that both of us seek to get universal health care.

I have a substantive difference with Senator Clinton on how to get there.[15]

As history now testifies, a centerpiece of Obamacare was indeed the very type of mandate for which candidate Obama so frequently criticized his primary opponent. Many, myself among them, believe such a mandate is unconstitutional—that you cannot force, under penalty of law or wage garnishment, individuals to purchase a commodity they do not want and still remain within the constraints the framers of the Constitution wisely put upon the reach of the national government. I believe that when this question reaches the Supreme Court of the United States, that mandate provisions of Obamacare will be struck down. (Or will if there remains a majority on the Court that believes that what the Constitution actually says matters.)

They say the past is prologue. Perhaps that is why, shortly after the President's victory in November, I found it a little jarring to hear the news that Rahm Emanuel had been selected as the Chief of Staff for the incoming administration. I knew a bit of the past. Rahm Emanuel had served in Congress with me since 2003 and, of course, was the fellow freshman who had taken it upon himself to do some assertive rearranging of the subjects at our photo session. Previously he had worked in the Clinton campaign and administration, followed by a brief season in investment banking that made him a multimillionaire. Known for aggressive-bordering-on-ruthless tactics, he had been the architect of the Democratic takeover of the House of Representatives in 2006. He had a reputation for hard work, but also a reputation that he would stop at nothing to achieve his goal. Certainly if there was ever a politician who operated by the credo, "the end justifies the means," it was Rahm Emanuel.

So it was a surprise to few when, a few weeks after the November election, Emanuel responded to a question on one of the Sunday morning news shows by saying, "Rule one: Never allow a crisis to go to waste. They are opportunities to do big things."

Without a doubt, as the Obama team prepared to take control of the Executive Branch of our government, they had big things in mind. And based on everything I had seen and heard during the campaign, I assumed some sort of government take-over of health care was one of the "big things."

I assumed the Obama team knew exactly what kind of legislation they wanted to see and how they planned to make it a reality. But when I look back now upon the way the health care legislation that eventually became law evolved over the first twelve months of the Obama presidency, it seems clear that they were not nearly as far along in their thinking as I had assumed.

One early indicator leading me to believe that Obama planned to ram a health care bill through the Senate as quickly as possible was his naming of former Senate majority leader Tom Daschle as the new head of the Department of Health and Human Services. I was unaware of any particular expertise that Mr. Daschle had with health care or the delivery of same, but he clearly had great experience with delivering legislation through the Senate, and that was precisely what would be required for an ambitious remaking of America's health care system in the image of Canada or the U.K. But within a few weeks, Senator Daschle's confirmation became enmeshed in some difficult tax evasion questions and his withdrawal from consideration rapidly followed.

Shortly before the election, the chairman of the Senate Finance Committee produced a white paper that I thought would be the basis for the Obama health care bill. Indeed this paper was produced after convening an all day meeting at the Library of Congress with various stakeholders in the health care debate, and it was my assumption that there must have been wide acceptance of the concepts discussed in this paper.

To my surprise, however, the approach laid out in that white paper never really gained any traction and is now just an obscure footnote in the story of health care reform's tortuous, convoluted path to passage.

That is not all I was wrong about. I also assumed that during the transition from the Bush to the Obama administration, we would see significant pieces of the health care proposal rolled out for public inspection—especially given all of the talk I had heard from the Obama campaign about transparency. Again I was mistaken.

In that same Democratic Primary debate in Austin cited previously, Senator Obama took pains to opine that Hillary Clinton's big mistake in her first attempt to nationalize America's health care system back in the first year of her husband's first term was not conducting the process out in the bright sunshine. Specifically, he said:

> One last point I want to make on the health care front. I admire the fact that Senator Clinton tried to bring about health care reform back in 1993. She deserves credit for that.
>
> But I said before, I think she did it in the wrong way, because it wasn't just the fact that the insurance companies, the drug companies were battling here, and no doubt they were. It was also that Senator Clinton and the administration went behind closed doors, excluded the participation even of Democratic members of Congress who had slightly different ideas than the ones that Senator Clinton had put forward.
>
> And, as a consequence, it was much more difficult to get Congress to cooperate.[16]

Given this kind of rhetoric, I assumed the folks on Team Obama would be committed to transparency and input as they moved forward on creating their health care legislation. As I said, events would reveal that I was mistaken. And if I had any lingering doubts about this, they evaporated when I heard Speaker Pelosi say of the 1,000-page bill no one had been given adequate time to read, much less study, "We have to pass the bill so that you can find out what is in it."[17]

Based on those (faulty) assumptions, I was sure that immediately after the new Congress was sworn in in early January that the committees would be presented with a fully developed prototype of the Obama plan in the form of a bill—the one I felt sure they must have been keeping under wraps for several months. Wrong on all counts.

"Maybe everyone is just too busy preparing for the week long self-congratulatory inauguration celebration to bother with health care legislation," I told myself. So I adjusted my expectations and looked for it to come in the week following the inauguration. In fact I was somewhat surprised that there was not more detail in the President's inaugural address regarding his plans for health care. But I can't honestly say I came away from the speech with a shred of additional understanding of the President's vision for health care in America.

The next three months saw very little activity as far as health care reform on the Democrats part. It was actually during this interval that I thought our side might do well to try to get out in front of this issue and at least lay down some principles around which meaningful health care reform could be structured. To say that I was not successful in making this argument to my side would be an understatement. But in fairness there were other battles going on dealing with the President's stimulus bill and the Democrats omnibus bill which taken together resulted in $1.3 trillion of spending. There was also climate change legislation that was being developed in both houses and of course the President and congressional Democrats still had considerable momentum from the election.

In early May, Senator Kennedy (D-Massachusetts) and Senator Max Baucus (D-Montana) sent a letter to the President stating that they would have health care legislation ready to present to the country in about a month's time. And true to their word, Senator Kennedy's committee did make public in the middle of June and announced that the "mark up" process would begin immediately. What this indicated, among other things, is that the old warhorses in Congress intended to be the ones in the driver's seat now that they sensed a once-in-a-century opportunity. It also became clear that these grizzled veterans expected the fresh young president to sign off on whatever they came up with. And indeed that is precisely what happened.

Along with the release of the Kennedy-Baucus bill was a preliminary budget scoring from the Congressional Budget Office. The CBO's estimate revealed a price tag over ten years in excess of $1 trillion for an approach that would provide coverage for only 13 million people who had previously lacked health insurance. Frankly, those numbers stunned me. You will recall that the Democrat's own constantly cited figure for the uninsured was 47 million. It seemed to me that if the American people were going to be asked to pony up an additional trillion dollars (in the first decade alone) for a program, they had every right to expect it to cover more than 13 million people.

What followed was one of the most astonishing displays of financial and mathematical wizardry I've ever observed. Numbers were adjusted, spreadsheets were filled out, provisions were carved out, and eventually the Senate committee produced a bill with a cost under $1 trillion and coverage numbers that reflected some improvement over the original estimates.

This was accomplished, in part, by proposing a form of health insurance that resembled a state Medicaid plan—one which could provide coverage for many more individuals at a total cost of $60 billion a year, or $600 billion over the ten-year budget window. This, in fact, was very close to the estimate that we had received in our committee back in September 2008 when asked to describe the low end of the cost of providing insurance to America's uninsured. The Senate mark-up continued, and later in the month of June the Senate health committee reported out its bill, which then had to go to the Senate Finance Committee for final adjustment.

In the meantime, right at the end of June, the House of Representatives took up and passed by a very narrow margin a climate change bill that, like the Senate's health care proposal, carried enormous costs and, therefore, a significant number of new taxes. Because the margin of passage on this so-called Cap and Trade Bill was so thin, there was considerable arm-twisting involved in getting the requisite number of representatives to vote in favor of the bill. Following that vote, late on a Friday, Congress adjourned for the Independence Day recess. Members of Congress were unprepared for the wrath of their constituents back home after they passed what seemed to be an ill advised energy bill in the middle of what still was a very harsh recession.

This represented only the first of several waves of "Town Hall" encounters that would become the bane of Democratic lawmakers throughout the summer. Members returned after the one-week recess significantly chastened by the wrath of their constituents. And indeed many Democrats from conservative districts resolved to think twice before they followed their leadership down a similar path with the health care bill. And Republicans who had voted with the Democratic majority were particularly singled out for criticism at home in their districts. They had learned first-hand the danger of siding with the Democratic Speaker of the House against the will of their districts.

In the spirit of not letting a perfectly good crisis go to waste, it appears that the grand Obama-Emanuel-Pelosi-Reid plan for the first year of Democratic control of both the White House and Congress called for passage of Cap and Trade legislation quickly followed by enactment of an ambitious, revolutionary health care bill. Unfortunately, that cold constituent slap in the face during the Fourth of July recess took all the wind out of the sails of the of the Cap and Trade bill. This also meant it was becoming increasingly difficult to round up votes for the health care legislation when it was eventually presented. The speaker had planned to have the bill through the three committees of jurisdiction by the middle of July, and pass the bill on the floor of the House prior to the August recess. But you know what they say about "the best laid plans . . ."

We are often told that it was Republican obstructionism that made passage of the health care bill difficult. But in fact nothing could be further from the truth. The Democrats had an enormous vote advantage on us in the House of Representatives. Furthermore, they had never hesitated to use this majority to pass other pieces of their agenda, whether there was any Republican support or not. If the Democrats had been unified, they could have followed Speaker Pelosi's plan to the letter. But in the aftermath of the public's wrath about the energy bill, no Republican was likely to stray over into that dangerous territory, and too many Democrats were also asking for a pass on voting in favor of another unpopular, budget-busting measure. The result was they simply did not have the votes to pass their bill. Yet.

The strategy then evolved into blaming Republicans, and subsequently Republican obstructionism, for keeping this wonderful new program from the American people. The truth was, because of genuine fear on the part of seven Democrats in my committee of Energy and Commerce, passage of the bill was significantly delayed.

What ensued was an extraordinary frenzy of arm-twisting, coercion, and incentivizing through promises and pork. Where those tactics didn't prevail, outright punitive threats were applied to the reluctant and resistant. Eventually enough of the so-called "blue dog" Democrats eventually capitulated, and late on the night of July 31, 2009, the committee passed its version of Obamacare with three Democrats still voting against it.

Congress then adjourned, and began what will likely go down in history as the most consequential August recesses of the last 100 years.

The Summer of Our Discontent had begun.

CHAPTER SEVEN

THE HEALTH CARE REFORM BILL

How Did *This* Happen?

LET US REVIEW THE FACTS: DURING CALENDAR YEAR 2008, THE LAST YEAR of the Bush administration, the debate was heating up for the next presidential election. The previously hot topic of the war in Iraq was beginning to recede, and as the last two months of the campaign arrived, a significant recession was shaking the economy. Exploiting just such a recession, the presidential campaign of Barack Obama gained the upper hand and really never looked back.

During the spring of 2008, when Obama was in the active part of the campaign for the Democratic nomination, he took the bold step of rejecting the notion of an individual mandate for health insurance. This of course had been the centerpiece of the Hillary Clinton campaign, but because this idea made labor unions nervous, he had abandoned this approach, except in the case of children.

Obama's health care platform also stipulated that every uninsured American should have coverage under the Federal Employees Health Benefit Plan, the type of insurance held by members of Congress. The cost realities of this approach were actually highlighted in a hearing in my committee on Energy and Commerce. The estimated cost for ensuring all uninsured Americans under the FEHBP was $800 billion per year. Another cost projection was provided that gave every uninsured American coverage under Medicaid, and that price tag was $60 billion per year. That works out to $600 billion over the ten year budgetary window. (Ironically, these numbers were actually much more in line with what the health care bill actually cost.)

During the fall of 2008, a famous meeting was convened over at the Library of Congress by the Senate finance committee and various stakeholders in the health care reform debate. Senator Baucus produced a white paper as a result of this meeting, and it seemed for all the world that this stance would be championed by the Democrats in their new health care bill.

So I was somewhat surprised that no health care bill was introduced after the election or indeed before or after the inauguration. An unfortunate taxation issue derailed Senator Tom Daschle's selection for Health and Human Services Secretary and this actually forced a hiatus for health care reform for several months. During this interval, I thought the Republicans might be able to gain the upper hand in the debate by introducing their own proposals, but the Republican leadership could not be convinced that this was a good idea. They preferred to wait until Democrats had their proposal and then react to it. We actually lost an opportunity to carve out a leadership role for our side after the Democrats had gone dark on this issue.

Well, maybe not completely dark. In January of 2009, around the time that the president was being sworn in, I created a policy group called the Congressional Health Caucus, largely as an outlet for my frustration with not having a role in either crafting policy or articulating the opposition. I was not allowed, as a member of the minority, to schedule hearings in my committees or subcommittees. I was not allowed to choose which witnesses were called when the Democrats did schedule these, and I had very little role—or at least, so I thought—in what our side would put forth as an alternative.

* * *

So, using the Congressional Health Caucus, I scheduled forums on what I considered to be the most important issues. I held off–the-record member briefings with thought leaders in healthcare, and at the staff level we provided information to communications staff in member offices about how to talk about healthcare from a Republican, or conservative perspective.

I set up a Website called HealthCaucus.org, and every forum that was held was webcast via this Website, and every webcast that went out is now archived on the Website so members can refer to such arcane topics as 'reconciliation' or 'medical loss ratio' if the need arises. Also in the days leading up to the vote, we put out a daily fact sheet on issues relating to the pending legislation, and of course continue to maintain a blog about what lies ahead.

In May and June of 2009 there were a series of meetings at the White House with six of the major stakeholders and the President. The American Medical Association, the American Hospital Association, America's Health Insurance Plans, the medical device manufacturers, pharmaceutical companies, and the Service Employees International Union were all involved in these discussions. In fact, in a much publicized photo op, each of the participants proclaimed that they had saved $2 trillion for reform of the health care system. Just what did this mean? From what data was the $2 trillion figure derived? Who gave up what? Who got what in return? It turns out no one at the White House would respond to those questions, so I filed what is known as a "Resolution of Inquiry" to get that information. Unfortunately, I was blocked by my Committee Chairman and the Administration. Eventually, we were told in spite of the publicity about this rather staggering sum, no one had made any notes at these meetings. There was no exchange of any emails as a result of these meetings. In fact, a $2 trillion agreement was apparently made based upon a handshake. Or a wink.

* * *

In June of 2009 both Senator Ted Kennedy and Senator Max Baucus wrote a letter to President Obama informing him that their committee work would soon begin. Indeed, Senator Kennedy's committee did introduce a bill which the Congressional Budget Office found to cost over $1 trillion but would only cover 13 million of the uninsured Americans. Needless to say these numbers were significantly disappointing. Cost and coverage numbers then became the focus of the health care debate. After that, every committee took great care in getting a score from the Congressional Budget Office lest there be unfavorable publicity because of either high cost or low coverage numbers. Nevertheless, the Senate Health Education and Labor Committee continued its work and subsequently reported out a bill in late June.

Over on the House of Representatives side of the Capitol, the month of June was punctuated by the forced passage of a very contentious Cap and Trade Bill. This passed by a very narrow margin on almost a party line vote just prior to a recess that began at the end of June. As members returned to their districts for this recess, they were met with a constituency that was outraged by the passage of this bill. Many members of the House of Representatives were unprepared for the anger directed at them for having passed what appeared to be a very controlling and expensive piece of legislation.

The Speaker of the House had intended to pass the health care bill on the House floor prior to the end of July. This trajectory was apparently planned in order to get the bill through quickly, before people had a chance to actually inspect it. What was labeled the "tri-committee bill", a bill that would be marked up by the Education Labor Committee, the Ways and Means Committee, and the Committee on Energy and Commerce, was introduced in mid-July.

My committee, the Committee on Energy and Commerce, was given one week to work on the bill by adding amendments. Each of the other two committees was given twenty-four hours. The thought of legislation that is this sweeping and had such a profound effect upon the future of America to have such a brief time for perusal and changes is almost unprecedented. Committee members who have been around for a while recalled that when the Clean Air Act passed in the early '90s, there was an eight-month markup in committee. The very brief time we were given to work on this bill seemed absolutely preposterous.

Nevertheless we proceeded with the work in my committee. I prepared fifty amendments to try to improve bill. We did not get the entire week to work on the bill, because seven Democrats were nervous about the size and scope of the bill, and they withheld their support. This caused the chairman of the committee, Henry Waxman, to recess the committee for four days while he worked on wavering members. The numbers on our committee obviously favored the Democrats, as they held the majority of seats in Congress. However seven Democrats defecting from the chairman would have meant that our side could prevail on any vote. Indeed that is just what happened on a relatively inconsequential vote early in the amendment process and the chairman promptly recessed committee. When we eventually did reconvene there was still a great deal of dissatisfaction on the Democratic side with what was described at the time as" the public option."

Ultimately enough Democratic members were convinced to vote with their party, and the bill passed out of our committee very late on the night of July 31 by a very narrow margin. In the end four Democrats did vote with the Republicans. This was not enough to stop the bill, but it had delayed the bill. Right after the vote the August recess began, and as a consequence of the delay, America got a good look at the 1,000 page monstrosity that the Democrats rammed through the three committees.

The August recess was unlike anything anyone had ever seen and many of us felt that when Congress resumed its work in September that there would be an opportunity to pause or rewind or rethink this bill. This was not to be the case. The President met with the joint session of Congress in the middle of September and told us it did not matter what the American people said, we were going to proceed with health care reform because essentially he and the speaker knew best, and the American people could safely be ignored in this process.

The fate of the bill as it left the three committees is interesting. Each committee has amended the bill several times—in fact five of my fifty amendments had been accepted. The bills all went over to the Speaker of the House, where the speaker, with heavy input from the White House, combined all three bills. Throughout the month of October, I continually asked members of the Democratic leadership when I would be able to see and read the bill.

At one point I was told to "read a good mystery instead." On another occasion: "We don't want you to read the bill." I suppose this is understandable, because if I had an opportunity to read the bill before the House would be required to vote on it, I would be a more articulate spokesman against it.

A reoccurring strategy as this bill marched from committee process to signing ceremony was the almost desperate attempts by the Democratic House leadership to keep their members insulated from their constituents. We were required to remain in Washington for the week leading up to the vote, even if that vote were to occur on the weekend. Telephone communications between the district and the Washington offices became difficult as switchboards were overloaded and perhaps even shut down.

In March of 2010, during the week before the final vote, I conducted several telephone town halls with constituents back in my district. Each night I would contact between 10,000 and 15,000 households, briefly update the progress of the bill, and then ask for comments. Invariably I was inundated with responses that expressed very real concern that the pending bill was either an overreach, unnecessary, or a federal government intrusion into an area in which it had no business.

Also at that time I participated as a "special guest" with an outside group called the Independent Women's Voice with telephone town halls they were doing around the country. Again during the introduction, the group's sponsor, Heather Higgins, would talk briefly about her organization, emphasize that IWV was sponsoring the call, mention that they had a doctor and a congressman on the line to talk about the bill and turn it over to me. I would introduce myself as a member of Congress, and a physician in my former life, from Texas. I would observe that many people had strong feelings for or against a pending healthcare legislation, and many had tried to contact their member of Congress but were unable to do so, and I offered myself as a "listening ear" if they had feelings they wanted to share with Congress. And share they did. They were upset about the bill. They were upset about the process by which the bill was coming forward. They were upset that they had been unable to talk to their own member of Congress about their feelings. They were livid that Congress was proceeding with this very critical piece of legislation with no involvement from the average citizen.

I did this on several nights leading up to the passage of the bill. It was not as if I had much else I could be doing, as again we were sequestered in Washington, D.C. during that time. And certainly no one from the Democratic leadership was reaching out to me, asking me for my insight as to how to make this a better product. So I applied myself where I thought I could provide the most help, which was talking to my Texas constituents, and to regular people throughout the country about what was happening to their healthcare for the future. I became more and more convinced that the bill as it was laid out, as people understood it, had serious opposition from at least 70 percent of the country.

This was further emphasized on the weekend when the vote was finally taken. Easily 20,000 to 30,000 people showed up at a rally outside the Capitol to vociferously show their opposition, but ultimately in early November, the House did pass the bill.

As a doctor, I found it significant that the American Medical Association remained intransigent in its support for this bill, even though America's doctors stood to gain little from it. Specifically a correction of the Medicare payment formula (a formula that is very detrimental to doctors), and medical liability reform were both missing from this House passed bill. In fact, on the Saturday we were to vote on the bill, I spoke with the fall AMA conference via telephone for their luncheon meeting and argued that they should rethink their position. Ultimately they chose not to alter their position and left their support for the bill intact. I'm convinced this played a big role in its final passage.

After the passage of the House bill things were quiet on our side of the Capitol for a while. The Senate continued to tinker with their committee results and ultimately began the process of writing a bill on which the Senate would vote. This actually occurred over the Thanksgiving holiday when the Senate bill first made its appearance. While the rest of the country was worrying about Thanksgiving and Christmas, the Senate continued to work on their bill. Many parts of it were extremely unpopular with the Democratic senators, and it required a great deal of arm twisting and vote buying to get to the sixty votes that would be required to pass this bill. Finally they were able to co-opt enough senators and the bill famously passed on Christmas Eve.

I will be forever convinced that no one in the United States Senate really knew what was in this bill that was passed hastily on Christmas Eve as a snowstorm was bearing down on DC. The senators were desperate to get home and simply patched together a bill which they all thought they could improve at some later date. I'm firmly convinced no one in the Senate ever expected this bill that they threw together late in the night before Christmas to become law, but unfortunately that is exactly what happened.

Normally after the House passes a bill and the Senate passes a bill, a conference committee would be convened. But while most members of Congress were out-of-town, members of the House and Senate were meeting trying to put together a new bill, which would then be passed. Since sixty senators had voted for what by all appearances was a significantly flawed bill, I am certain it was felt by the Democrats that if they put together a better product, sixty senators would indeed vote for its passage.

The second weekend in January it appeared that they were very close to achieving this ideal. In fact, the President of the United States came to the Democratic retreat in the Capitol Visitor Center to convince wavering members that they must compromise on a combined product. News reports coming out of the Capitol that weekend seemed to indicate that the final hurdles had been breached and the new compromise legislation would soon be introduced.

Then something happened that no on expected. The following Tuesday in the state of Massachusetts, the Senate seat formerly held by Teddy Kennedy was won by the Republican candidate for the United States Senate. This caused great confusion on Capitol Hill amongst Democrats.

They appeared absolutely disoriented and were unsure of how to proceed. The easiest thing for them to do would be to quickly pass the Senate bill in the House of Representatives, thus making the Senate bill the law of land.

And here is some interesting information. HR 3590 was not a health care bill when House passage first occurred in the summer of 2009; in fact it was a housing bill. But in order to get a House-passed vehicle for the Senate bill, the housing bill was amended by the Senate to remove all of the housing language and health care language was inserted. Thus we had a health care bill, which had been passed by both houses. All that would be required for the bill to go to the President for his signature would be for the bill to come back to the House of Representatives and concur with the Senate amendment. While this was openly talked about by several individuals in those days following Scott Brown's election, no one really thought that this would happen because the Senate bill was such a poorly constructed product. In fact, at one point the Speaker of the House said that she did not have 100 votes in the House of Representatives for the Senate bill, so poor was the construction of this piece of legislation.

How this thing then got from dead-on-arrival to a presidential signing is something that will be debated by the ages. There is no question that the President's appearance at the retreat likely played some role, as did the subsequent appearance of Republicans and Democrats at the Blair House for a joint meeting. The unprecedented snowstorms that paralyzed Washington for several days also played some role in at least allowing the Democrats additional time to catch their breath and plot strategy.

But during the two weeks before the vote was actually taken, more and more Democrats in the House of Representatives were threatened, co-opted, or otherwise brought into line by the Speaker of the House of Representatives, the White House, and members of the administration. There were continued grumblings from rank-and-file members on the Democratic side that they were being coerced by the White House into accepting this piece of legislation. In fact one conservative Democrat famously remarked, "They can break my arms, they can break my legs, but I am not voting for this bill."

But unfortunately not every member of the Democratic conference had the resolve of this individual. When it was finally down to just a precious few, wheeling and dealing became hot and heavy and of course, the ultimate decision by a pro-life Democrat to accept the abortion language contained in the Senate bill—which really provided no protection from the use of federal funds for paying for abortion—occurred, and those last few Democrats were firmly in the palm of the Speaker of the House.

Again the Capitol was surrounded by at least 30,000 Americans voicing strong opposition to what the government was doing with this bill. At the end of the day this was not enough. The Speaker had the votes and the bill passed and went down to the President for his signature.

Because of all the problems contained within the Senate bill, a bill to correct some of the technical deficiencies was passed under reconciliation language. This allowed the technical corrections package to be passed with only fifty-one Senate votes, and it had no difficulty achieving that mark.

As you can see, no one really knew what was in this bill when it was passed, because the Senate bill was never intended to become law. My theory is that this was a placeholder bill which was passed hastily by the Senate to get them out of town on Christmas Eve, and the Senators assumed that they would be able to come back to make major adjustments in the legislation. Because the public was repulsed by all the deals that were cut in order to get the bill passed, popular support, which had never been high, sank to an all time low with the election of a Republican in Massachusetts. This created stark fear in the Democratic conference, and they decided to push the bill through regardless of the consequences. That unfortunately leaves us where we are today, with most people uncertain as to what the future holds, and even experts in disagreement about what the ramifications of this legislation actually are.

CHAPTER EIGHT

HOW THE NEW LAW AFFECTS YOU AND ME

ARTICLES IN VARIOUS MAGAZINES AND NEWSPAPERS HAVE ATTEMPTED TO do side-by-side comparisons and timelines of what people might expect. Realistically, the rules and regulations written by career federal employees in the Department of Health and Human Services and other agencies such as the Internal Revenue Service are what will determine the road ahead. No one really knows what the future holds. Suffice it to say there is little solid ground that people can find at the present time, and people are looking for answers.

Here are my conclusions on the ramifications of this very unsound legislation.

- With the passing of this bill, for the first time in the history of the United States of America, there now exists a mandate stating that every man woman and child be required to purchase a product: health insurance. If an American does not maintain an insurance policy that person may be fined $325, or 2 percent of their income whichever is larger. These fines do increase over time. Thus a family that earns $80,000 a year and does not purchase health insurance would be subject to a $1,600 a year fine—PLUS that family would still be uninsured. *NOTE: Many states are looking at court challenges to this individual mandate because it does seem like such an excessive reach of federal power.*

- There is a great deal of discussion as to whether people will lose their current insurance. Many people are concerned that if they have a high deductible health plan, for example, or even some employer-sponsored insurance, they may not be able to keep the products that they have grown comfortable with over the years. In spite of the repeated mantra during the debate over this bill—"if you like what you have, keep it"—the fact is that nothing could be further from the truth.

- In 2012, the amount of medical costs that may be deducted from a person's tax liability will change from 7 1/2 percent to 10 percent of total medical expenses. New taxes on medical devices will start in fairly short order. These changes are likely to have wide ranging consequences and the results will reverberate for years.

- Another result is a vast expansion of Medicaid. Medicaid is a state and federal partnership. Indeed, Medicaid is a contract between the state and federal governments about insuring low income Americans. The federal government has now altered that contract significantly without any input by the states. This does raise a question as to whether or not the states will be required to go along with the federal government on this huge change to Medicaid. What is unclear, but seems entirely likely, is that anyone who earns less than 133 percent of the federal poverty level will in fact have no option but to be covered by Medicaid. That means no private insurance will be available to this group of the population—for instance, a family of four making less than $29,500.00 in 2010—unless they happen to be in the country illegally.

- If your insurance plan costs too much money it may also be taxed. There will be a new payroll tax for Medicare as well as a 2.9 percent tax on certain medical devices. One of the great ironies is that leeches and medical maggots will be subject to this tax.

- There will be an $8 billion a year fee on the insurance industry. One can assume that this $8 billion will not come from CEO salaries and lobbyist expenses but just simply be passed on to ratepayers. Do the math.

- The federal share for safety net hospitals, those that provide care to low income, uninsured Americans, will be reduced year-over-year. Interestingly, in a state like Texas where a great number of the uninsured are in the country illegally and without the benefit of a Social Security number, and since the President has said that no illegal aliens will be covered under this plan, there likely will still be a significant number of people left uninsured.

- There will be a reduction in the number of dollars that are available for what are called Medicare advantage insurance policies. Currently 25 percent of America's seniors are covered under Medicare advantage plan and will see their level of service decline because of these cuts.

- There will be a cap on home health expenses, and some $80 billion will be cut from this program over the next ten years.

- Health savings accounts or high deductible health plans will likely not be able to survive this transition. Those plans are a powerful instrument in holding down costs as well as preserving patient autonomy, but because they're unlikely to be deemed qualified plans by the Secretary of Health and Human Services, they will probably no longer be available to American citizens. This may be the single most pernicious aspect of this legislation.

SOME IRONIES AND EMBARRASSMENTS

- While still open to some interpretation, most people understand the bill to say that members of Congress and their personal staff can be covered only under the newly designated insurance exchanges. Since none of these exist until the year 2014, a literal reading means that all members of Congress and their staff are now uninsured. While it is possible this will quickly be corrected by designating the Federal Employee Health Benefits Plan as an exchange, but it has been the cause of some concern, however ironic.

- Interestingly, senior committee staff, leadership staff and members of the administration and their staff are excluded from this requirement. Of course, it was the senior committee staff and the staff of the administration who wrote large portions of this bill.

- The heart of the bill was supposed to provide coverage to children under age eighteen with pre-existing conditions. It turns out, the language of the bill does indeed provide for *prevention* of pre-existing conditions but not funding for coverage of those individuals. Also insurance companies, while they may not exclude children with pre-existing conditions, are free to charge whatever premium they feel is justified in this setting. News reports indicate a willingness on the part of the country's insurance companies to work with the administration to solve this shortcoming, but this is just one major error in a bill that now has the President's signature.

BIG PICTURE CHANGES

- The passage of the bill gives the Secretary of Health and Human Services unprecedented power. Never before in the history of this country has this amount of power over the lives of everyday

Americans been held by a single agency head. The Secretary may now require a certain type of insurance to be purchased, disallow some insurance types, and may dictate what procedures and treatments may be available to patients and likewise may be able to prohibit procedures and treatments as well. Of course, changes or prices will be determined by the Secretary.

- The group of six special interests, what has been referred to as the Bake Sale Six—hospitals, doctors, insurance companies, medical device manufacturers, pharmaceuticals, and unions—all work together to craft secret and special deals with the White House. In spite of what the President himself said would be the most open and transparent process this country has ever seen, none of the information from those special deals will be made available to the American people because the special interests do not *want* the information made available.

- Massive changes are taking place in the realm of electronic health records now. The future of data management and comparative effectiveness evaluations are likely to play a huge role in this government run system that is now being created. No one should be against gathering data or accurate data, but we should be concerned about whom will be using this information and how it will be used. Currently there are very few controls over what the government may have planned in this regard.

- A rather expensive fix to a mistake in the physician payment formula is still unsolved. This is likely to cost between $200 and $400 billion more than what the advertised price tag has been on this massive health care reform.

- One of the more dangerous aspects of the bill as passed is the creation of a new Board that will recommend cuts in Medicare to Congress. Congress will only be able to vote up or down on this package of cuts, and will not be able to modify the package that comes forward. This so-called Independent Payment Adjustment Board will have broad new powers and almost no accountability to

America's seniors. It truly is one of the more concerning aspects of this legislation as it goes forward.

■ Here's a simple truth: In Medicare the number of patients are going to increase in the coming years—the so-called baby boom demographic. The cost and complexity of care will increase as medical science advances. And yet there is going to be $500 billion in savings from Medicare in order to pay for this new insurance entitlement to cover the uninsured. How to resolve these two disparate concepts seems to be something that has been totally ignored by the bill writers. How is cutting over $1000 a year from current Medicare recipients going to provide more or better care in future years, when the number of recipients is projected to grow so rapidly? Indeed, projected savings from Medicare expenses is likely to be little more than smoke and mirrors in order to get a budgetary answer that was desired by the bill's authors.

CHAPTER NINE

MALIGNED AND MISUNDERSTOOD:

Scapegoting Doctors and Insurance Companies

It was Edward Zwick, the acclaimed maker of war movies who said, "I think it's too easy often to find a villain out of the headlines and to then repeat that villainy again and again and again. You know, traditionally, America has always looked to scapegoat someone as the boogie man." This is not a new political impulse, of course. It goes back at least as far as Nero's attempt to deflect public anger over the fire that destroyed much of Rome in A.D. 64 by casting suspicion upon the Christian minority in the city.

One centerpiece of the campaign to drum up grassroots support for the Democrat's health care overhaul was the attempt by President Obama and his allies in Congress to fan the flames of resentment, first against doctors, and when that failed to get traction, against insurance companies. And if you are still losing, blame "Republican obstructionists".

At the height of the battle over health care reform, the other side made much of the fact that the prestigious American Medical Association (AMA) had endorsed the House proposal. The proponents hoped the American people would interpret the endorsement to mean that the majority of doctors were in favor of the measure. In fact, the AMA did not speak for most doctors; an overwhelming majority of doctors were opposed to the measure; and in the end, the American people made no such assumption.

In the interest of full disclosure, I am a dues-paying, active member of the AMA. In fact the only other elective office I have ever held was as an alternate delegate to the AMA. As much as I value the reputation of the AMA, as much as I believe in their mission—to advance the art and science of medicine—it was painful to watch the implosion of yet another organization where the leadership was on a different page from the membership. Apparently a tone deaf leadership is not a problem exclusive to the United States Congress.

It is not widely known that only about 15-20 percent of doctors are members of the AMA. A better indicator of physician sentiment in that period came from Sermo.com—a 115,000-member, online community of doctors. In November of 2009 the folks at Sermo released polls showing that 92 percent of doctors did not think the Democratic bills addressed the "real sources of cost increases," and 94 percent did not believe "effective" health reform was possible without tort (liability) reform—something our Republican approach included but the Democratic bills did not. A Sermo poll from earlier in the summer revealed that 94 percent of physicians opposed the various Democratic approaches to health care change; and, by the way, 95 percent said that the AMA didn't speak for them.[18]

In fact, during the markup of the health care bill in Committee on Energy and Commerce, where I offered some fifty amendments, I was constantly thwarted by my chairman, Henry Waxman, who would patiently explain to me that the bill had already been endorsed by the AMA, and as a consequence my amendments were unnecessary.

Nevertheless, there was a concerted effort by those pushing the House and Senate versions of a health care overhaul to make it seem as if most doctors thought the idea was wonderful. At one White House news conference/photo op, 150 doctors were invited to the Rose Garden to demonstrate their wild enthusiasm for Obamacare. The physicians had been instructed to bring white lab coats to wear for benefit of the television and newspaper cameras. Several, however, forgot or refused to bring a lab coat. White House interns were quickly dispatched to round up white coats for these folks. Rahm Emanuel and company were determined to manage the "optics" of their campaign to sell Obamacare to the American people. White lab coats made appearances at several congressional press conferences as well.

In the end, these theatrical presentations seemed to backfire, as much sport was made of these photo ops because doctors rarely wear lab coats outside of their offices. For many, what was supposed to appear impressive came off as contrived and out of context.

Oddly enough, several months before this coordinated effort to present doctors as being compassionate caregivers fully on board with the Democrat's proposals (whether the doctors liked it or not), a very different strategy had been pursued—one that sought to whip up grassroots support for Obamacare by painting doctors as greedy, heartless, fat cats. Early on it was clear that most doctors in the nation were not onboard and were becoming increasingly vocal and organized in their opposition. Thus, before there was a strategy of presenting the doctors as wise allies in the fight for reform, there had been a season in which they were painted as greedy impediments to progress.

One of the first shots in this effort to cow the medical community into silence came in the form of a broadside from Representative Jim McDermott (D-Washington), a psychiatrist by training. In an interview with Fox News Channel, McDermott suggested that doctors were throwing around phrases such as "socialized medicine" to scare people into opposing the President's plan. He said, "The doctors who have responded this way exhibit a serious case of doctor greed. They have lost sight of the common good and the pledge they took in the Hippocratic Oath."[19]

Firing back, Dr. George Watson, a Kansas physician and president of the American Association of Physicians and Surgeons said, "This is war. This is a bureaucratic boondoggle to grab control of health care. Everything that has been proposed in the 1,018-page bill will contribute to the ruination of medicine."[20]

Around the same time, President Obama stepped personally into the fray to advance the strategy. For example, in a rare prime time televised news conference on July 22, 2009, President Obama, in the middle of a long, rambling answer to a question about the public option provision said, "Right now, doctors a lot of times are forced to make decisions based on the fee payment schedule that's out there. So if they're looking and you come in and you've got a bad sore throat or your child has a bad sore throat or has repeated sore throats, the doctor may look at the reimbursement system and say to himself, 'You know what? I make a lot more money if I take this kid's tonsils out.'"[21]

The response from the medical community was swift and incredulous. The following day, a *Wall Street Journal* editorial headlined, "Dr. Obama's Tonsillectomy" noted:

> If that's what he really thinks is wrong with U.S. health care— and with the medical profession—then Obamacare is going to be even worse than we thought. The point Mr. Obama oversimplified is that the way the U.S. pays for medical services can encourage some physicians to prescribe unnecessary tests or treatments, especially in Medicare. But his implication is that doctors aren't acting in the best interests of their patients in order, basically, to rob them.[22]

This is exactly right. But the editorial board could have also pointed out that the primary driver of unnecessary testing and treatments in medicine is not greed but rather fear—specifically fear of being sued. In the days that followed the President's press conference, physicians, physician's assistants, and nurses across the nation rose up to point out the false assumptions and faulty logic behind the President's statements. Lydia, an incensed physician's assistant in Bloomfield Hills, Michigan wrote the *Wall Street Journal*, declaring:

> I am stunned by your editorial "Dr. Obama's Tonsillectomy" (July 27). It is simply beyond comprehension that the chief

architect of health-care reform, President Barack Obama, has no clue about the medical decision-making process and no confidence in the ethics of physicians.

Primary-care providers do not "make a lot more money" by recommending tonsillectomies; they don't even perform the surgery. We would make a referral to an otolaryngologist or pediatric surgeon based on medical necessity—not fees. We would be the normal conduit to the physician performing the surgery . . . If this is the way the White House thinks, we desperately need some real medical professionals advising President Obama. But then, we are all busy actually taking care of patients.[23]

Another letter to the editor brought forward the perspective of the surgeons actually doing those tonsillectomies. Dr. Gerald B. Healy and Dr. Edward M Copeland III, both past presidents of the American College of Surgeons, wrote:

President Obama stated that surgeons look at fee schedules and make decisions about patient care in order to make more money. This was an unfortunate and false characterization of the thousands of dedicated men and women who render surgical care across this country every day. Some of this care is rendered without reimbursement as "free care." Reimbursement for surgery has fallen steadily for the past several years, while malpractice premiums and office costs have risen. This has led to early retirements and a steady loss of qualified surgeons, especially in rural America.

America's surgeons will always strive to do better, but at this moment we are the standard for the world. It is unfortunate that the President chose to make off-handed and invalid comments about physician motivations for care at a time when we should all be working together to improve America's health-care system.[24]

Undeterred, the President continued to press this line of attack for a few more weeks. Perhaps the "unnecessary tonsillectomies conspiracy theory" didn't get traction because the surgery was too benign. So, in a televised town hall meeting in Portsmouth, New Hampshire, Mr. Obama seemed to suggest that, because of financial incentives built into the current system, doctors were not vigorously treating patients with diabetes and therefore preventable amputations were routinely performed. He said:

> All I'm saying is let's take the example of something like diabetes, one of—a disease that's skyrocketing, partly because of obesity, partly because it's not treated as effectively as it could be. Right now if we paid a family—if a family care physician works with his or her patient to help them lose weight, modify diet, monitors whether they're taking their medications in a timely fashion, they might get reimbursed a pittance. But if that same diabetic ends up getting their foot amputated, that's $30,000, $40,000, $50,000— immediately the surgeon is reimbursed. Well, why not make sure that we're also reimbursing the care that prevents the amputation, right? That will save us money.[25]

As with the tonsillectomy example, there was immediate pushback. The American Association of Orthopedic Surgeons voiced its opposition to the remarks in an open letter to the President. Their letter pointed out that Medicare reimbursement to physicians for foot amputations is nowhere near "$30,000, $40,000, $50,000" but rather ranges from approximately $700 to $1,200, including follow-up care provided by the surgeon for up to ninety days after the operation. The letter also pointed out that, along with numerous other organizations, AAOS had previously testified before Congress that chronic delays in reimbursement by Medicare and other payors were creating additional paperwork burdens that in turn hampered their ability to care for patients.

The "demonize those rich and greedy doctors" strategy backfired spec-tacularly. The reason for this, I believe, is that people tend to know their doctors personally. He or she is not a faceless, nameless corporation or special interest. He is the guy whose daughter plays on your daughter's soccer team. Or she is the fellow parent you see at school functions. People generally know, like, and trust their doctors and don't begrudge them decent compensation and a good living given the years of education and expense required to become a physician.

All of this explains why the proponents of radical health care reform quickly changed targets. The insurance companies that faced being regulated out of business made a much better bogeyman. After all, just as almost everyone likes their doctor, almost no one likes their insurance company. Indeed, at some point during the chaotic, tortuous process to pass their legislation, proponents of health care reform stopped calling it that and began referring to it as "insurance reform."

Now before I continue, it might be helpful if I define a couple of terms that were thrown around frequently during the months-long debate over the nation's health care future. The first is the phrase "single-payer system." This refers to a health care system like that of Great Britain in which all health care payments come from the government. The vast majority of doctors, nurses, and other health care providers working in the U.K. are essentially government employees—working for a huge agency called the National Health Service (NHS). A single-payer system such as this can accurately be described as *socialized medicine*, although proponents hate it when you call it that. As I pointed out in Chapter 2, such systems tend to suffer from severe shortages of doctors because the rewards are limited and working within a government bureaucracy is often maddening.

Technically, the United States already runs several "single-payer" health insurance programs—Medicare, Medicaid, the Veteran's Administration health care system, and the fairly new State Children's Health Insurance Program (SCHIP). But these plans only cover specific segments of the U.S. population. When most advocates of a single-payer system use the term, they are speaking of a *universal* program that would cover every person in the nation.

The other frequently heard term was a "public option" component in the health insurance legislation. This phrase is shorthand describing the establishment of a government-run, taxpayer-subsidized insurance program for people whose employer does not offer health insurance and cannot qualify for or afford private health insurance. In other words, some versions of health care reform provided for the establishment of a federal health insurance agency to compete with the established private companies. Thus, in these schemes, people could choose traditional private insurance or choose the governments "public option." I wanted to explain these concepts because, as the public relations war for the hearts and minds of the American public regarding health care legislation heated up, and the focus shifted from doctors to insurance companies, those terms were flying around constantly.

While "Operation White Lab Coat" was still winding down, Speaker Pelosi launched the new strategy on July 30 as she was taking questions from a group of reporters on Capitol Hill. As a Reuters' reporter described it, "Pelosi on Thursday ramped up her criticism of insurance companies, accusing them of unethical behavior and working to kill a plan to create a new government-run health plan."[26] But she was just getting warmed up. "It's almost immoral what they are doing," the Speaker thundered. "Of course they've been immoral all along in how they have treated the people that they insure. They are the villains. They have been part of the problem in a major way. They are doing everything in their power to stop a public option from happening."[27]

This was astonishingly strong language coming from the person third in line to the Oval Office. It is difficult to recall another major political figure characterizing an entire American industry as "immoral all along" and "villains."

And just what were the insurance companies doing that invoked the wrath of the Speaker? Essentially they were pointing out that a piece of legislation designed to ultimately drive them out of business would . . . well, ultimately drive them out of business. Numerous knowledgeable individuals from outside the insurance industry had been pointing out for some time that if Congress included a so-called public option in the final version of the health care bill, that it would eventually lead to the major insurance companies, one by one, abandoning the health insurance business due to unfair competition from the government.

This was precisely the conclusion reached by Heritage Foundation fellow John Hoff in a white paper he released a few weeks after Speaker Pelosi's incendiary accusations against the insurance industry. In it, Hoff points out that any government-sponsored insurance plan would be likely to capture a large portion of the market and, in the process weaken the standing of the private insurance companies. Hoff concluded:

> Coupled with the federal regulatory system that the legislation would impose on the remaining private plans, this would clearly by itself constitute a government takeover of health care.
>
> Even worse, the federal takeover would accelerate. The private plans' relatively small market share would likely render them increasingly uneconomical and lead to a death spiral in which private insurance would serve an ever-decreasing share of the market.
>
> In short, the federal insurance plan is a giant step toward the single-payer system that the President has admitted that he prefers. The single payer would be the federal government. This would create a nationalized health care system much like those in Europe and Canada.[28]

At the time of these debates, one of the dirty little secrets in Washington was that the public option provision was indeed merely a transitional half-step on the way to what had long been the progressive dream of a single-payer, universal system of health care in America on the model of the British or Canadian system. And it wasn't just opponents of the public option saying this. When some advocates of the public option were speaking behind closed doors to liberal groups that were hoping for full-scale socialized medicine, they often encouraged those groups to get behind the public option plan—even though it was far short of the universal program they wanted—assuring them it would ultimately lead to one.

For example, in early 2009 Representative Jan Schakowsky (D-IL) was speaking to a group called Health Care for America Now—an umbrella organization networking more than 1,000 left-leaning organizations favoring universal health insurance coverage. A recording revealed that she told the audience: "And next to me was a guy from the insurance company who argued against the public health insurance option, saying it wouldn't let private insurance compete; that a public option will put the private insurance industry out of business and lead to single-payer. My single-payer friends, he was right. The man was right!"[29]

A YouTube video posted in July of 2009 shows a member of a group called Single Payer Action ambushing Congressman Barney Frank and asking him why Congress doesn't just start all over on health care reform with a Canadian-style single payer plan. Congressman Frank's answer is revealing:

> I think that if we get a good public option it could lead to single-payer and that is the best way to reach single-payer. Saying you'll do nothing till you get single-payer is a sure way to never to get it. . . . I think the best way we're going to get single-payer, the only way, is to have a public option and demonstrate the strength of its power.[30]

Even more revealing are the remarks of liberal Washington Post columnist Ezra Klein to a convocation of left-leaning online activists called "Netroots Nation" in July of 2008. Asked by an audience member about the Democrats approach to health care reform which, to this audience, seemed too weak and watered-down to merit their support, Klein reassured the group by spilling the beans: "[The proponents of health care reform] have a sneaky strategy, the point of which is to put in place something that, over time, the natural incentives within its own market will move it to single-payer."[31]

Contrast those frank admissions before friendly audiences to what President Obama told a gathering of the AMA in June 15, 2009. After acknowledging that some people had "legitimate concerns" about his proposal, he added:

> What are not legitimate concerns are those being put forward claiming a public option is somehow a Trojan horse for a single-payer system. . . . So, when you hear the naysayers claim that I'm trying to bring about government-run health care, know this—they are not telling the truth."

The President's reassurances notwithstanding, the concerns about the public option seemed pretty "legitimate" to the major health insurance companies. And in the light of the comments noted above, it is obvious that the insurance companies were not crazy or delusional to suspect that any approach to health care reform that included a public option provision was destined—whether intentionally or simply through the law of unintended consequences—to put them out of business in the long run. Likewise, a huge segment of the American population felt that no matter how frustrated or annoyed they were with the insurance industry, it was lunacy to think that the federal government was going to do a *better* job. Indeed to believe so would represent a massive triumph of hope over experience.

When the majority of Americans looked at the enterprises currently run by the federal government (Medicare, the IRS, the Social Security Administration, etc.), or entities that had been granted a monopoly by the government (the U.S. Postal Service) they saw no reason to believe that yet another government-run entity was going to be a model of efficiency and good service.

Nevertheless, one of the common criticisms of the insurance companies is that they are basically heartless brutes who denied claims at every opportunity (and most likely laughing, rubbing their hands together, and twirling their moustaches while doing so). Fortunately, someone thought to wonder at what rate the existing government insurance company, Medicare, was denying claims. According to the American Medical

Association's "National Health Insurance Report Card," Medicare denies 6.85 percent of its claims. Guess what. That is higher than any private insurer. That rate of claim denial was more than double that of any private insurer's average.[33]

Now no one who knew me during my decades in medical practice ever mistook me for a big fan of health insurance companies or HMOs. Indeed insurance is the bane of most doctors' existence. The pleasure of practicing medicine would increase a hundredfold if we could go back to the simple old days before health insurance—the days of country doctors in which we all paid for services as we went, and the local doctor usually provided an unofficial, seat-of-the pants sliding scale of fees based on the patient's ability to pay--which sometimes meant getting paid in chickens, garden vegetables, or barter. Of course, that was long before the days of MRI machines, minimally invasive surgeries, and gene therapy. As treatment technologies have exploded, costs have soared commensurately. The advancing complexity of what we are able to do in medicine is an enormous cost driver. And those costs must be paid by someone, somehow.

Back in the late 1980s, I once got so angry with an HMO medical director during a phone conversation in my home that I lost my temper, got into a shouting match on the phone, and used some colorful language. He demanded the immediate discharge from hospital of a new mother who had delivered the day before. It was her second child, and according to his HMO guidelines, that patient only "got" one day in the hospital before her discharge was required.

Only one problem—she was also deathly ill from an aggressive viral gastroenteritis, and dehydration from the ensuing vomiting and diarrhea coupled with the blood loss from the delivery made her significantly more unstable than the average postpartum patient. I had been up with her all night and most of the day (it was a Saturday) trying to get and keep things under control. I had finally gotten home, dog tired, worried, upset, and concerned that I had abandoned my family one more time when he called.

"She has got to be discharged," he told me.

"I'm sorry—she can't, she is not stable. It would not be safe," was my reply.

"Her coverage only allows single day after her delivery," insisted the medical director.

I went on to explain her symptoms and that this was not a routine case.

"I don't care," was his reply. "You know the rules—and that means a one day postpartum stay for a multigravid patient."

Growing angrier by the minute, I gave him a detailed and graphic description of her gastrointestinal symptoms and finished with this flourish, "and I'm not convinced that this is only a viral gastroenteritis, for all I know this could be (expletive) cholera."

He was unmoved—"Well I assume she has at least one toilet in her house—she will manage fine."

Clearly we were talking past each other at this point. Finally he said firmly, "Dr. Burgess, either you go back to Lewisville Hospital right now and discharge the patient or I want your resignation on my desk the first thing Monday morning."

"I certainly will not discharge the patient; it is not medically wise to do so. But let's not wait until Monday. Tell me where you are right now and I will bring you my resignation . . ." and I think I went on to describe how such resignation might be most appropriately delivered.

I slammed down the receiver, shaking with rage, and looked over to see my two young children, eight and ten years old at the time, their eyes wide and brimming with tears. They heard the whole thing and were quite traumatized by it. "Dad, did you just get fired?" My daughter asked.

I quickly came into focus, dropped to one knee and with my arm around both said as calmly as I could, "No honey, I am self-employed—no one can fire me but myself. And I think I have had enough of that particular HMO, but do not worry there are plenty of others." I get tears in my own eyes to this day when I think about that incident. And I have always wondered if the ugliness of that moment contributed to their decision not to pursue medicine as three generations of the Burgess family had before them.

It's one thing to get frustrated at insurance companies and wish they better understood the needs of doctors and patients. It's another thing to demonize them and work for their replacement by yet another inefficient, corruption-fostering bureaucracy. But then demonizing the insurance companies is nothing new. They have long been a target in America. A prime example is documentarian Michael Moore's 2005 film *Sicko* which, in classic Moore style, presented the insurance industry in evil caricature. At the New York screening of this film, Moore candidly said: "We have to eliminate the private insurance companies. They have to go."[34]

That's a radical statement, but it is likely to generate a good number of "amens" among almost any group of American citizens. As I've already observed, we're a polarized nation, but hatred of insurance companies appears to be something around which we can all come together, hold hands, and sing. But there is one problem with all that. For several hundred years, insurance companies have performed a vital function in the great economies of the world and have played a vital role in the progress that has raised living standards all over the developed world.

Even so, it seems that a lot of Americans, and an even greater percentage of politicians, don't understand the basic economics of insurance. For legislators, that's like bridge builders not understanding the laws of physics—in other words, dangerous for all involved.

All insurance, whether it is auto, home, life or health insurance, is built upon the concept of *shared risk*. Take 1,000 homeowners. Let's assume that the statistics show that one and only one of those home owners is likely to experience a large fire in a ten year period of time. But individually, none of them can afford to rebuild their homes should they happen to burn down. The problem is, none of them know if they are the one-in-a-thousand that is going to experience the loss. The good news is, they can pool their risk—sharing the individual risk across the entire group by paying monthly premiums into a risk pool fund—and agree that when one of them experiences a fire, the fund will cover their loss. That's shared risk.

Whether it works in the real world or not depends on two things: (1) how good the insurer is at calculating the level of risk, and (2) using that knowledge to determine the appropriate premium every member has to pay into the fund to keep it solvent. The likelihood of success increases if those who have chosen to live in more fire-prone areas or who have demonstrated themselves to be careless with fire, pay a little more than their wetter, safer fellow members.

Speaking of fire, the concept of shared risk actually has its origin in the aftermath of the Great London Fire of 1666 in which 13,200 homes were lost. The following year, as the city was rebuilding, English doctor and businessman Nicholas Barbon applied the logic I described in my crude example above and created the world's first fire insurance company. He collected small premiums from a large pool of property owners, invested the funds for growth, and paid claims out of that fund.

Less than a hundred years later, on this side of the pond, Benjamin Franklin brought the practical application of shared risk theory to American soil. He founded the Philadelphia Contributionship for the Insurance of Houses from Loss by Fire in 1752. The company offered perpetual insurance against fire. Instead of charging periodic premiums, Franklin's company accepted a single deposit from the insured. The company agreed to pay any losses during the term of the policy. When the insured cancelled the policy, the company returned the deposit to him or her. In the meantime, the company earned profits by investing the deposits.

For shared risk to work, the premium amount cannot be an arbitrary number. If the insurer charges too little, it will not be able to pay its claims. If it charges too much, it will not be able to compete in the marketplace. Premiums are based on actuarial science, balancing expected losses against expected earnings. Having an adequate fund to pay anticipated claims is called an "actuarial balance." The public option would have ignored the issue of actuarial balance—assuming all the risk without distributing the costs. Or in reality, passing the costs along to future generations in the form of debts and deficits, just as we're currently seeing with Medicare.

I have great respect for the office and the person of the President, but to be honest, at many points throughout the debate over what the President started calling "insurance reform" I got the distinct impression that neither he nor Speaker Pelosi or Majority Leader Reid really understood any of the realities I just outlined above.

For example, Obama in a single breath once criticized insurance companies both for refusing to insure high-risk people and for not keeping rates low. Huh? If an insurance company insures more high risk people and doesn't raise premiums, it will eventually become insolvent and unable to pay anyone's claims. An insurance company can hold premiums down by limiting its risk and being selective in whom it insures; or it can accept all comers by charging ever higher premiums. The immutable laws of mathematics demand that it has to be one or the other, even if the President of the United States decrees that he must have both.

The fact is, premiums are rising dramatically because the underlying health care costs those premiums must cover are rising dramatically. The real question is: Why is the cost of getting well and staying well rising sharply year after year? It's a question on which I attempt to shed some light in Chapter 11.

And as bad as some insurance companies were fifteen or twnety years ago, many have come a long way in the interval. Some of the newer products that contain High Deductible Health Plans coupled with a Health Savings Account are much more patient and doctor friendly. In fact many now include preventive care with no additional out-of-pocket expense, monitoring patients with a personalized Electronic Medical Record and providing e-mail reminders of when preventive care or screening visits are due.

I currently have such coverage, and my health insurance premiums are about one half that of comparable PPO coverage. And since I pay less for coverage, I can put some of those savings into my Health Savings Account. True, I do not have coverage for prescriptions, and yes, there are a few medications that I do take on a regular basis, but I pay for these medications with a debit card that draws on my Health Savings Account. In effect I am using pretax dollars for these expenses. And of course I am a much more cost conscious shopper since I'm spending my own money.

For now, it is important to realize that what President Obama, Speaker Pelosi, and many others who were blasting the insurance industry as a way to drum up support for "insurance reform" were demanding was clearly in violation of the laws of physics and economics. And what Speaker Pelosi described as "immoral" and villainous was really just rational business practice reflecting the underlying problem of soaring medical costs.

Some of the arguments I heard from my colleagues in support of creating yet another government-run insurance program was that pooling demand would drive costs down. But as a clear-headed article by a Connecticut health insurance consortium pointed out in the middle of the debate, "Health care is not one of those industries that benefits from economies of scale."[35] The article goes on to point out:

> Dumping 20 to 40 million new patients into the health care system will not make it more efficient. On the contrary, the sudden influx of the newly insured will create a logistical nightmare.
>
> . . . Eventually, inevitably, the public option health program will face an actuarial crisis, just as Medicare does today. As the rolls of the public option swell, so, too, will the costs. Because the risk is not shared proportionately, the system will face deficits, becoming another unfunded entitlement. The funds required to keep this bloated program afloat will cost the taxpayer even more than private health insurance. By then, however, private health insurance companies will be out of business. There will be nowhere else to turn.[36]

In spite of these realities, the health care debate rolled on in 2009 and into 2010 with two different versions of the bill ultimately under consideration—one in the House and the other in the Senate. The House version of Obamacare contained a provision for establishing a public option insurance program. The Senate version did not. But in both houses of Congress and at the White House, insurance companies and doctors' groups continued to be vilified if they criticized either of the bills.

For example, on February 20, 2010, Secretary of Health and Human Services Kathleen Sebelius seized upon the announcement by a network of Blue Cross/Blue Shield health insurance providers that they had to raise premiums. She took the news as an opportunity to issue a report melodramatically titled *Insurance Companies Prosper, Families Suffer: Our Broken Health Insurance System.*[37] Given the title, I was somewhat surprised not to see a picture of Snidely Whiplash tying a defenseless damsel to railroad track on the cover of the report.

In a press conference touting the new report, Secretary Sebelius blamed the rate increases on excessive profit-seeking on the part of insurance companies and called a number of companies out by name, particularly Anthem Blue Cross in California, Anthem of Connecticut and Anthem of Maine, Blue Cross/Blue Shield of Michigan, Regence Blue Cross/Blue Shield of Oregon and Blue Cross/Blue Shield of Rhode Island.[38]

President Obama took up the theme a few days later during his weekly radio address. He too called out Blue Cross/Blue Shield of Michigan.[39] There was just one small problem with these criticisms. The three Blue Cross Blue/Shield insurance companies from Michigan, Rhode Island, and Oregon—the ones that were supposedly money-grubbing profiteers raising rates—were *non-profit* organizations. Not only are these companies structured as not-for-profit entities, they are heavily regulated by their respective state governments. Blue Cross-Blue Shield of Michigan, for example, is required by state law to accept all applicants. And as we've already seen, if an insurance risk pool *must* take high risk or high cost members, then premiums for all members of the pool must rise, otherwise the pool becomes insolvent.

The inconvenient truth undermining Sebelius' and Mr. Obama's full-throated denunciations of these insurance companies was that the state-regulated non-profits and for-profits were both increasing premiums and in similar ways. In other words, the insurance companies weren't being evil. They were being rational.

With both the House and Senate versions of the bill seemingly stalled in their respective legislative chambers, Mr. Obama exploited the flap over the Blue Cross/Blue Shield premium increases as an opportunity to introduce his own bill. It represented a blend of the two approaches but leaned more toward the model of the Senate bill. By March, the White House had strong-armed or "incentivized" enough legislators and the House took up and passed the Senate Bill without amendment.

As we're about to see, however, in the months that followed its passage most of the negative outcomes about which I and a bipartisan group of opponents to the bill warned during the debates, began to come to pass with a vengeance.

CHAPTER TEN

LEGISLATIVE
MALPRACTICE

On March 23, 2010, President Barack Obama sat at a table in the East Room of the White House surrounded a large group of beaming, back-slapping, high-fiving politicians and special visitors. The eighty-four-year-old John Dingell was seated beside him. Another 300 dignitaries were packed into the room, 200 or so of them lawmakers. Twenty-two commemorative pens were arrayed on the table before him and he used each of them to sign portions of the sweeping Patient Protection and Affordable Care Act into law.

A few minutes earlier, the East Room had been a cross between a pep rally and a victory celebration. Waiting for the President to arrive, the crowd broke into call-and-response cheers, with one group shouting "Fired up!" and another replying with "Ready to go!" When Speaker Pelosi had entered the room, the crowd erupted in cheers and began chanting, "Nancy! Nancy! Nancy!"

A few minutes later the President and Vice President Joe Biden came striding into the room, and the already raucous crowd erupted and leapt to their feet. Once the group quieted, Mr. Biden took to the microphone to formally introduce the President. As Biden finished his introduction, applause and cheers in the room rose to a roar once more as Biden stepped back to shake the President's hand. Forgetting he was wearing a press microphone, the Vice President leaned into the President's ear and said, "This is a big f****** deal."

Locker room language aside, he was right. It was a big deal. Unfortunately for our country, not in a good way.

Here we were, scarcely more than a year after a global liquidity crisis had come perilously close to bringing the world's banking system down; mere months after the deepest economic recession in several generations had bottomed out; and only weeks into a very weak and fragile economic recovery. At this moment the President and his allies were enacting legislation that would add crushing new paperwork burdens to businesses, pile new taxes, fees, and fines onto individuals at various levels, and expand the reach of government in ways no one could fully predict.

In the months preceding the signing, public opposition to the bill had grown. Ironically, the Democrats had begun the process of introducing health care reform legislation immediately after the election of Barack Obama by citing polls and claiming that the majority of Americans were demanding it. That may or may not have been true as long as "health care reform" was a vague, theoretical concept. But theory had become reality. And the fact was, the more individual Americans learned about the implications of Obamacare, the less they seemed to like it. Indeed, in the week prior to passage of the bill, ten separate surveys of public opinion were conducted to gauge the citizenry's stance on the bill—phrasing the questions in a variety of ways. Not one of those ten polls revealed a majority in support of Obamacare. Three of the surveys showed the nation equally divided; the other seven indicated either a majority or a plurality of Americans in opposition.[40]

As a personal aside, another irony of the vote is that I was directly warned by more than one of my Democratic colleagues that those of us who opposed the bill would face the wrath of an angry electorate if we voted against it. I was told that Republicans would pay a high price in the

2010 election for standing in the way of something the American people were demanding. As history now records, that is not precisely how the elections of 2010 turned out. Although, they were correct about that voter wrath thing.

Finding out precisely what the bill called for proved to be a challenge. Republicans were effectively locked out of the process of crafting the bill. Once we got a look at the product, our problems weren't over. It wasn't just that the bill itself was well over 1,000 pages long. Those pages contained hundreds of references to other existing pieces of legislation that this bill would modify or nullify. To truly understand the impact one had to find the referenced statutes and read those as well. At one point, Speaker Pelosi made her now-famous remark to an audience, "We need to pass the bill so you can find out what's in it."

They did pass it. And in the months since, all of us, including many who voted for it without remotely understanding what they were foisting upon the nation, have been finding out, revelation by revelation, what was in it. It hasn't been pretty, in spite of the fact that, as of this writing, many of the provisions of the legislation haven't even been phased in yet. There is worse, much worse, yet to come.

As is now increasingly apparent, the drafting and passage of the Patient Protection and Affordable Care Act represents an act of gross legislative malpractice. Before I point out some of the worst effects of the bill itself, allow me to point out some of the worst aspects of the process that created the bill. If the process was rotten, it is difficult to expect the product to be anything but defective. The question for the ages: was this gross incompetence, or premeditated malevolence? In either case, disaster looms.

For starters, the President and his allies in congress paid lip service to our nation's desperate need for entitlement reform while forcing a massive new entitlement program on the nation. Instead of having the courage to grapple with the twin looming fiscal catastrophes of Social Security and Medicare, the creators of Obamacare chose to create a third one.

Equally cynical were the hyper-partisan legislative tactics used as well as the arm-twisting and vote-buying. (Remember the Louisiana

Purchase and the Cornhusker Kickback? Who can forget Gator-Aide and UConn?)

Finally, the leadership of the House and Senate shut Republicans out of any meaningful role in writing health-care legislation, killing any possibility of producing a bipartisan bill. Toward the end of the process, at the much-hyped Health Care Summit at which the President agreed to sit down with Republican and Democratic lawmakers, he spent the majority of the time talking rather than listening. On top of all that, key elements in the legislation are very likely unconstitutional and will certainly be tested in the courts.

No matter how the sausage was made, it has now been served to the American people. What follows are some examples of the unhappy outcomes our nation has experienced thus far as a result of the passage of Obamacare.

LESS COVERAGE, FEWER COVERED, AND FEWER CHOICES

During the debate, several of my colleagues and I were concerned that under the new law, many businesses that had been providing paid health insurance for their employees would no longer be able to do so, and that many insurers would be forced to stop offering certain types of policies while others would simply withdraw from the market all together. Sadly, this is exactly what has happened immediately after Obamacare's provisions began to come online.

For example, almost immediately after passage, many insurance companies that had previously provided children-only policies were forced to stop offering them, due to unfeasible mandates on such policies embedded in the bill. This form of policy had been filling a vital gap for working parents and single parents who received health coverage through their place of employment that did not extend to their children; and for parents who could not afford health insurance for themselves but wanted their kids covered.

Unfortunately, after the insurance companies got a look at the new requirements for such policies, they quickly realized they could not comply and remain solvent. So, being rational, companies all over the nation announced they would no longer be offering such policies.

By October, the Obama administration was backtracking on those provisions of Obamacare and Health and Human Services Secretary Sebelius was announcing, in so many words, that those provisions that were frightening off the insurance companies would not be enforced. (For now.)

This brings up one of the key drawbacks of such huge, complex government regulatory schemes. They create a lot of room for bureaucratic discretion on the part of regulators and therefore a lot of room for offering preferential treatment to your friends, allies and supplicants. It also gives the government regulators a stick with which to threaten those who don't go along to get along.

That's why throughout the debate, many of us who opposed Obamacare argued that the legislation would empower the Executive branch to show favoritism and create an unlevel playing field for businesses.

Those fears were validated in October of 2010 when the Department of Health and Human Services announced that thirty corporations, among them McDonald's, Jack in the Box, and a New York teachers' union, would receive exemptions from a rule that would have required them to raise the minimum annual benefit in their employee insurance plans.

Without those special exemptions, the rule would have compelled these companies to drop their employee coverage; leaving almost a million workers without the insurance they had before the passage of health care measure that was supposedly born to solve the problem of *uninsured* Americans.

The problems with this are many. For one thing, these "waivers" are only good for a year. The companies that received them will be forced to go back to the government, hat in hand, year after year. (When it comes time for those corporations to consider making political and philanthropic donations, is it possible this annual supplication to the Executive branch will not factor into management's thinking? "Best not annoy the party in power if we want to get our exemption.")

Secondly, the granting of such waivers is unfair to the thousands of smaller companies who don't have the lobbying clout in Washington, D.C.

to get one for themselves. As Yuval Levin, a fellow at the Ethics and Public Policy Center, wrote about the granting of these waivers:

> . . . these companies now need permission from the administration to offer their employees a benefit they have offered for years. And of course, many other companies—those without the lobbying operation of a company the size of McDonald's, or without the access to liberal policymakers that a NY teachers' union has—can't get the same permission, and so can't compete on a level playing field, or offer coverage that might entice the best qualified people to work for them. This kind of government by whim, and not by law, is the essence of the regulatory state. We are about to see a whole lot more of it—unless the health-care law enacted in March is repealed.[41]

If you are the owner of regional chain of hamburger restaurants, your government has now put you at a competitive disadvantage to McDonalds and Jack in the Box, loading you with burdensome costs that you must either bear or pass on to your employees. Either way you lose.

All this centers around only one of the thousands of new regulations embedded in Obamacare, of which most of the provisions, at this writing, have yet to be implemented.

Of course, it is not just types of policies disappearing under Obamacare. Within a few months of passage, some companies announced they were getting out of the health insurance business altogether.

In September of 2010, the Principal Financial Group in Iowa announced it was leaving the medical insurance business. UnitedHealth Group will, for the time being, pick up Principal's 840,000 customers. The *Wall Street Journal* reported that Principal's exit from the health insurance market is, in part, because "smaller insurers will have a hard time competing with bigger players under the [Obamacare] overhaul."[42]

Around the same time, six other small insurance companies notified the Iowa Insurance Division that they were getting out of the health insurance business in Iowa, as well.

As insurers drop out, competition is reduced, which in the long run is always bad for consumers. Of course, the folks who crafted Obamacare had no interest in or little respect for the free market forces that tend to spur innovation, drive customer service, and keep prices in check. As we saw previously, the ultimate goal is the elimination of private health insurance altogether. Obamacare is only a transitional stepping stone toward universal health care coverage delivered via a government entitlement program. When enough insurers withdraw from the business of offering health insurance, a "crisis" in health coverage will be declared. And as we have observed, there are those who know one must never let a good crisis go to waste.

At that moment, the "public option" which died along way to Obamacare will be resurrected. Shortly thereafter, the rest of the private insurers will disappear, and the public option will be the only game in town.

All of this is inevitable unless the Congress or the courts are successful in undoing the damage done by this serious case of legislative malpractice. The good news is, the election of 2010 brought more doctors into Congress than ever before.

CUTS IN MEDICARE

One of the sad ironies of the passage of Obamacare is that its proponents consistently claimed that the legislation wouldn't affect Medicare, that on the contrary, if it didn't pass, drastic cuts in Medicare were right around the corner. These assurances and warnings were an effort to sway seniors, whom the polls showed were solidly against the measure (and for sound reasons).

In July of 2009, President Obama participated in a conference call hosted by AARP (American Association of Retired People), an organization that alienated a huge segment of its membership when it endorsed Obamacare. As a CNN story on the call reported:

> President Obama tried Tuesday to alleviate senior citizens' concerns about health care reform, saying his plan will maintain

Medicare benefits and allow people to keep the coverage and doctors they now have . . . Obama repeatedly insisted his plan would improve the value of spending on Medicare, so that the quality of coverage would remain the same while the cost would go down . . . "Nobody is talking about trying to change Medicare benefits," he said. "What we do want is to eliminate some of the waste that is being paid for out of the Medicare trust fund."[43]

Indeed, as of this writing, Medicare is on course to become insolvent in 2016, and the long-term unfunded liabilities of the program are more than $38 *trillion*. Obamacare's approach to defusing this ticking fiscal time bomb was to create savings in Medicare through more than half a trillion dollars in cuts to the program. These included billions in cuts to the popular Medicare Advantage program.

In reality, what the health care reform measure did was rob Peter to pay Paul. It drastically cut payments to healthcare providers in such a way as to force an impossible choice upon them—i.e., either stop seeing Medicare patients, or go broke. This is something that some of us who opposed the bill tried to point out at the time, but few in the left-leaning news media were interested in listening.

As predicted, this has already begun. The list of health care providers announcing they can no longer accept Medicare patients is growing daily. Thus a key result of health care reform is that access to health care is shrinking for millions of Americans. And this is before Obamacare's cuts to the Medicare Advantage program have even begun to kick in.

On September 28, 2010, Harvard Pilgrim Health Care announced that on the last day of that year it would be forced to drop around 22,000 Medicare Advantage customers in Maine, Massachusetts, and New Hampshire. As a spokeswoman for HPHC explained to the *Boston Globe*, "We became concerned by the long-term viability of Medicare Advantage programs in general."[44] She said the insurer also worried about Obamacare's requirement that it contract with physicians, rather than letting customers choose their own doctors.

As James Capretta, a Fellow at the Ethics and Public Policy Center, observed: ". . . the Medicare Advantage cuts will fall disproportionately on low-income and minority seniors who don't have access to a retiree wraparound plan and can't afford Medigap coverage. For them, the lower cost-sharing offered by Medicare Advantage plans is instrumental in helping them afford the care they need."[45] A study of this issue by Mr. Capretta and Robert A. Book concludes that 7.4 million seniors are likely to lose their benefits by 2017 under the current legislation.[46]

The math of all this is inescapable and the results were utterly predictable. Nevertheless, Secretary Sebelius stood before a group at an AARP convention of October 1, 2010, and stated that there would be "more" Medicare Advantage plans thanks to Obamacare, despite the law's significant cuts to the program. Upon hearing about the claim, Senator Charles Grassley challenged the Secretary Sebelius to back up that claim. Instead, the online transcript of Sebelius' speech on the HHS Website was quietly edited[47] to reflect her saying, "There will be more *meaningful* choices" and in another passages the term "more choices" was altered to read, "better choices."[48]

This is the same Secretary Sebelius who spent much of the debate over passage of Obamacare labeling opponents like me as sources of "misinformation" for accurately pointing out that the proposed law would increase health-insurance premiums—which is precisely what has happened since its passage. And this is the same Sebelius who, since passage, has attempted to cow insurance companies into silence about how the law is negatively affecting them and their policyholders.

In a September 9, 2010, letter to representatives of the insurance industry on Capitol Hill, Secretary Sebelius warned insurers that the administration would not tolerate their blaming premium hikes on the new health overhaul law. "There will be zero tolerance for this type of misinformation and unjustified rate increases," Sebelius warned. "Simply stated, we will not stand idly by as insurers blame their premium hikes and increased profits on the requirement that they provide consumers with basic protections."[49]

She went on to warn that punishment for criticizing the new law might come in the form of exclusion from new health insurance markets that will open in 2014 under the law—a potential market of 30 million individuals. This heavy-handed threat and authoritarian tone may have come as less of a surprise to those who took note of a Sebelius' comment during an ABC News Radio interview a couple of months earlier. Then she said, "Unfortunately, there still is a great deal of confusion about what is in [the reform law] and what isn't. So, we have a lot of reeducation to do."[50]

It was an unfortunate choice of words at best. The term *reeducation* sent a chill down the spines of many, particularly America's Vietnamese immigrants who recall fleeing the North Vietnamese "reeducation camps" set up after communist forces overran South Vietnam in the mid-1970s.

RISING PREMIUMS

As we saw earlier in this chapter, anyone who understands the very basics of how insurance risk pools work could see the lack of logic in Obamacare's promises of lower insurance premiums. As a law professor noted on his blog:

> You cannot add some 30 million to the pool and claim to reduce cost. You cannot define children as being up to 26 years old, keep them on mom and dads insurance policy, and reduce cost. You cannot force insurance companies to cover people with preexisting conditions and reduce cost. And the list goes on and on. Obama, Pelosi, Reid and the minions told us it would indeed save cost. After the law passed (of course), they are now saying it will do no such thing.[51]

In the months since the first provisions of Obamacare began to be phased in, health insurance premiums have risen across the board. These increases have frequently come not in spite of the bill's "insurance reform" provisions, but as a direct result of them.[52] But there is much more to come. Barbara A. Brody Associates reports that in 2011, Obamacare's restrictions will push health premiums up 30 percent in New York for singles, couples, and families with children.

In the beginning, we were all told that this bill was a vital solution to the problem of rising health care costs. But the fact is, this legislation did not reduce spending in health care. The CBO estimates the bill will increase overall health spending in the U.S. by $222 billion between now and 2019. What the bill does is shift rising costs from some favored groups and piles them upon others. That isn't reform. It's redistribution of wealth and wholesale enlargement of government.

As humorist P.J. O'Rourke quipped a few years back, "If you think health care is expensive now, wait until it's 'free.'"

SPIRALING SPENDING AND SOARING DEFICITS

Another promise made by the sellers of Obamacare that should have been greeted with at least universal skepticism if not hoots and howls of derision was that the measure would help reduce the deficit.

Indeed the "official" Congressional Budget Office estimate released three days prior to the bill's passage reported savings of $140 billion over ten years time. However less than a month later, Richard Foster, chief actuary for the Center for Medicare and Medicaid services released a report estimating that $318 billion would be added to the deficit for the same period of time. An almost $450 billion difference within less than a month. If you believe as I do that you must never attribute to coincidence that which can be adequately explained by conspiracy, you see that the previously described incompetence/malevolence equilibrium is clearly shifting in the direction toward malevolence.

In the debate running up to the passage of Patient Protection and Affordable Care Act, supporters argued that it would actually help reduce the nation's exploding budget deficit because the net effect of new taxes and fees, along with its extensive cuts in the Medicare Advantage program. Like most of the other promises that were put forth to sell this monumental boondoggle, this one too has proven to be empty.

It seems that the promoters of the bill had given the Congressional Budget Office deeply flawed assumptions about the levels of subsidies that would be necessary for lower income families under the plan. Just how flawed?

Well, in October of 2010, a study commissioned by pro-Obamacare group called Families USA revealed that in the first year of full implantation of Obamacare (2014), a full 28 million Americans were likely to be eligible for health care subsidies at a cost of more than $110 billion. This was more than six times the original Congressional/CBO estimate.[53]

The supposed deficit-reducing aspect of the Patient Protection and Affordable Care Act was shouted from the mountaintops by proponents and gave legislators cover in voting for it—allowing them to claim that it was the fiscally responsible thing to do. In the end, it was all smoke and mirrors. Common sense told the average man on the street that you simply can't provide more stuff for more people more of the time and "save" money. And they were right.

But it is not just the federal budget being busted by this legislation. In fact, a huge portion of the associated costs is simply being passed on to the states. Take Mississippi, for example. There Governor Haley Barbour hired a consulting firm to analyze Obamacare's impact on his state. "Their findings are staggering," Barbour told state legislators in a letter on October 8, 2010. He told state lawmakers that Obamacare "will result in a massive expansion of Medicaid, which is projected to cost Mississippi taxpayers up to an additional $1.7 billion over the next decade. I have grave concerns regarding how we will be able to fund other essential public services that our citizens need," Barbour wrote. "More money devoted to the Medicaid program means less funds will be available for public safety, state health clinics and hospitals, colleges and public schools."[54]

Meanwhile the governors of the other forty-nine states are also wrestling with how to manage the sobering impact of the health care reform bill's Medicaid mandates on their already stressed state budgets.

It's not just conservative "Red" states that resent the intrusion and cost. Oregon senator Ron Wyden wrote Oregon's state health director Bruce

Goldberg in August of 2010, encouraging him to seek a waiver from Obamacare's individual mandate.[55]

If Obamacare is so good for the nation, why do so many need a waiver from its provisions?

MORE BUREAUCRACY

The new law as currently written vests several government departments with new responsibilities and powers—particularly the Department of Health and Human Services and the IRS. But it also creates an astonishing array of new powerful boards and entities.

For example, Obamacare created something called the Independent Payment Advisory Board (IPAB) as part of its Medicare cost containment provisions. This fifteen-member panel now has the authority to enact cost-cutting changes in Medicare reimbursement without any additional approval from Congress. We are told the panel will apply something called "comparative-effectiveness research"—research that must be commissioned and paid for by the taxpayers—to determine what the most "cost effective" methods of treatment are for a health problem. Then, armed with that information, the board can deny Medicare reimbursement for treatments or therapies deemed less effective. In other words, for Medicare patients, health care decisions will be moved out of the doctor patient relationship and determined by a bureaucratic board, based on bureaucratic statistics. Unless, of course, the doctor wants to forgo getting paid. Or the patient wants to pay out of pocket, which incidentally is a violation of Federal law.

But this is one of only scores of new boards, panels, departments, and enforcement divisions created by the legislation. How many exactly? Sadly, no one can say for sure.

Two investigative journalists from the news site Politico.com, Gloria Park and Fred Barbash, have been working hard to get to the bottom of that important question. An article by the two writers titled, "Health Reform's Bureaucratic Spawn," begins:

> Don't bother trying to count up the number of agencies,
> boards and commissions created under the new health care law.
> Estimating the number is "impossible," a recent Congressional
> Research Service report says, and a true count "unknowable."[56]

As the authors point out in the article, the language of the bill actually leaves open the possibility of an unlimited supply of new agencies and bureaucracies. For lovers of big government, Obamacare will be the gift that keeps on taking.

Some who have attempted to get an idea of where the count begins have come up with the number 159. That's the number of "new bureaucracies, insurance mandates, and higher taxes" hidden in the complex law according to a study by the Republicans of the Joint Economic Committee.[57] The committee did us all a service in attempting to create a flow chart that visually reflects the staggering new array of boards and agencies and how their often-overlapping responsibilities and areas of oversight relate to each other. It is a poster filled to overflowing with scores of shapes connected by a hundreds of connecting lines spreading like spaghetti across the document.

When I look at that image, I am reminded of something Professor Thomas Sowell said: "It is amazing that people who think we cannot afford to pay for doctors, hospitals, and medication somehow think that we can afford to pay for doctors, hospitals, medication, *and* a government bureaucracy to administer it."[58]

INCREASED UNEMPLOYMENT AND PROLONGED RECESSION

The marketers of Obamacare tried a number of different pitches to the American people before simply giving up and just ramming it through Congress whether the American people wanted it or not. First it was the need to insure the fabled "47 million" uninsured Americans. At other times it was necessary to reign in, (pick one), (A) greedy doctors, (B) greedy insurance companies, (C) greedy hospitals, or (D) greedy physician-owned hospitals. (No mention of trial lawyers or plaintiffs seeking to get rich through non-meritorious lawsuits, however.) Nevertheless, the oddest and most surreal argument for Obamacare was the one made by the President and his allies suggesting that we needed to pass the bill for the good of "the economy." At times, it sounded as if the overhaul was going to serve as the ultimate stimulus program.

For example, in an April 2009 article titled, "President Ties Health Care Reform to Economic Recovery," the *California Healthline* newsletter noted, "In a speech at Georgetown University on Tuesday, President Obama said that health care reform and other priorities from his agenda are needed to build a stronger U.S. economy and that an overhaul should be enacted by the end of the year."[59] And a year later, shortly after passage of the health care bill, Speaker Pelosi wrote: "The budget conference report reflects President Obama's economic plan, a blueprint for economic recovery and new jobs now—and sustainable economic growth and prosperity for years to come. For the first time in years, we will have an honest budget that: creates jobs with targeted investments in affordable health care, clean energy, and education."[60]

There is an unbridgeable chasm between this sunny rhetoric and economic reality. The fact is, Obamacare is a jobs killer and a recovery killer. It exacerbates the deficit even while increasing the tax burden on middle class families. The Patient Protection and Affordable Care Act is undermining an economy struggling to claw its way out of the deepest recession in eighty years.

Validating this view is an October 2010, report from Senators Tom Coburn (R-OK) and John Barrasso (R-WY), both of whom are physicians like myself. Titled "Grim Diagnosis: A Check-Up on the Federal Health Law," the report from the two doctor-lawmakers draws on numbers from the non-partisan Congressional Budget Office and think tanks.

Before the health care legislation became law, proponents of the overhaul claimed that health reform would create jobs. At the White House health care summit in February, the Speaker of the House of Representatives asserted the federal health care overhaul would create "400,000 jobs almost immediately," both in the health care industry and "in the entrepreneurial world as well." However, recent independent reviews have contradicted such rosy scenarios and found the legislation will wipe out hundreds of thousands of jobs.[61]

As promised by the title, the twenty-seven-page report makes for grim reading. There is an entire section on the Congressional Budget Office's estimates for job losses directly resulting from the law; another connects the dots on how forcing employers to pay for health insurance will leave them no choice but to do less hiring; and a third segment exposes the way the law will further diminish the already shrinking job opportunities for young people.

The CBO released an updated "Budget and Economic Outlook" in August of 2010. It concluded that the health care law's aggressive enlargement of the Medicaid program would certainly incentivize some lower income individuals to work fewer hours if they realized that making a little more money would push them over the income threshold (400 percent of the poverty level) for the sizable subsidy offered through Medicare ($7, 830).[62] In other words, if you are a working parent earning just under four-times the current poverty level, and your boss offers you a promotion that will earn you an extra $5,000 per year, you will turn it down if you've done the math. That extra $5,000 will cost you almost $8,000 in lost health care subsidy.

The CBO calculates this effect will shrink the labor market by about a half-percent. That may not sound like much, but it equates to more than 788,000 jobs. That is more than the combined work force of GM, Ford, and Chrysler.

This isn't the only job-killing feature of Obamacare. There is a 2.3 percent excise tax on medical device companies that will push some struggling companies into unprofitability. Furthermore, the law now compels businesses with more than fifty employees to offer full-featured health insurance to every worker. How many rational business owners will be likely to consider hiring additional employees once they have hit that fifty-employee threshold? At that point, using contractors and other forms of outsourcing will become very attractive. Finally, the law's ridiculous ban on new doctor-owned hospitals has resulted in the cancellation of dozens of construction projects.

As pointed out previously, this bill also dumps massive responsibilities onto state governments at a time in which most state budgets are already reeling from recession-related revenue drops. Obamacare exacerbates this fiscal emergency by forcing states to expand Medicaid.

My home state of Texas alone estimates that the law will force them to spend an additional $27 billion on Medicaid from 2014-2023.[63] Nationally, these additional state budget burdens could run in the hundreds of billions of dollars. And these costs weren't factored into the CBO's estimates because they aren't technically federal expenditures. But taxpayers in the individual states *will* pay for them. And these are scarce budget dollars states will have to divert from spending on betters schools, better roads, repaired bridges, or economic development.

The sad fact is, the Patient Protection and Affordable Care Act leaves much of the law's dirty work, including establishing "exchanges" to limit the health-insurance choices of many of their residents, to the states.

DOCTOR SHORTAGES

Unless much or all of Obamacare is rolled back, get ready for the doctor shortage I warned about in Chapter 1. According to the Association of American Medical Colleges, that shortage could reach up to 150,000 doctors by 2025.[64] We were already facing an impending doctor shortage before this deeply-flawed bill passed. It was a problem I tried to address through a couple pieces of legislation I introduced in 2009, but couldn't get through Speaker Pelosi's congress. But the passage of Obamacare threatens to make that serious problem much, much worse.

Just a few months prior to the passage of Obamacare, a survey of doctors by The Medicus Firm, a Dallas-based physician recruitment agency, revealed that nearly one-third of 1,100 doctors surveyed indicated they would be considering a career change if Obamacare became law.[65] Medicus' analysis of the survey said, " . . . health reform could be the proverbial 'last straw' for physicians who are already demoralized, overloaded, and discouraged by multiple issues, combining to form the perfect storm of high malpractice insurance costs, decreasing reimbursements, increasing student loan debt, and more."[66]

A poll commissioned by Investor's Business Daily yielded similar results. It revealed that about two-thirds of doctors were opposed to Obamacare and a full 45 percent said they would consider quitting if it passed.[67]

As a pointed out in Chapter 1, severe doctor shortages in Britain and Canada have followed socialized medicine just as predictably as winter follows autumn. And in those countries, they have met that shortage by raiding poorer developing nations of their best and brightest—luring them away from their native countries where they are desperately needed.

The hard fact is, unless the rewards for practicing medicine begin to once again balance the expense, preparation, pressures, risks, liabilities, and bureaucratic hassles that currently characterize being a doctor, many of our own best and brightest will pursue other careers. And should progressives achieve their dream of single-payer, universal health care in a system in which doctors are essentially government employees, we will see an unprecedented mass exodus from the profession.

EROSION OF PROFESSIONALISM

Ezekiel Emanuel, MD, the physician brother of Rahm, who is an active if unseen hand in health care reform, recently published the following observation in an online version of *The Annals of Internal Medicine*: "To realize the full benefits of the affordable care act, physicians will need to embrace rather than resist change. The economic forces put in motion by the act are likely to lead to vertical organization of providers and accelerate physician employment by hospitals and aggregation in the larger physician groups. The most successful physicians will be those who most effectively collaborate with other providers." He later goes on to say, "These coordinating functions traditionally have been managed by hospitals or health plans. Only hospitals or health plans can afford to make the necessary investments in information technology and management skills."[68]

In other words, doctors should stop resisting the new world order of Obamacare and embrace it. Things would be better if doctors were employees of hospitals or insurance plans or the government. The argument among health policy types is that you cannot control costs unless you also control the doctors who are writing the prescriptions and ordering the tests and hospitalizing patients.

But what is wrong with this picture? The doctor is supposed to be the advocate for the patient, at least that is what I learned at my father's knee. If the doctor works for the hospital, or the health plan for that matter, or the government for that matter, to whom is he or she responsible? Either the hospital, the health plan, or government but certainly not the patient. And that results in a perverse alignment of incentives. Remember my story of my fight with the HMO medical director? I was able to stand up to him because I was a self-employed private practitioner. Were I a wholly owned subsidiary of the HMO would I have had the courage and/or the autonomy to stand up for my patient? I hope so, but the answer may not always be so clear when the physician is merely an employee of the institution.

EXPANSION OF ABORTION

Finally, I would be remiss if I didn't mention that Obamacare, if it remains intact as passed, will most assuredly result in a significant expansion of abortion in some states. The state health insurance exchanges established under Obamacare will unquestionably include plans that cover abortion and this constitutes a clever end-run around the spirit of the Hyde Amendment.

The Hyde Amendment is a longstanding legislative provision that bars federal programs from funding abortions with taxpayer dollars. Technically, these exchanges are run by the various states and therefore not subject to the restrictions of the Hyde Amendment. But Obamacare provides extensive federal subsidies of those exchanges. That means your and my federal tax dollars will be used to help fund insurance policies that pay for abortions, whether that violates our consciences or not.

In the final weeks of debate over Obamacare, some pro-life Democrats, such as Michigan's Bart Stupak, were reluctant to throw their support to the bill because it provided virtually no restrictions on abortion. For example, the Community Health Centers (CHCs) commissioned and funded by the legislation were free to do abortions all day long. President Obama tried to assuage these concerns, and was largely successful in doing so by promising to issue an Executive Order expressly prohibiting such activities by the CHCs. Pro-life advocates pointed out that Executive Orders can be changed at any time. An EO was nothing nearly as ironclad as having actually pro-life language in the bill.

The bill contains several other open doors for federally funded abortions in the legislation, including the bills "high-risk pools," and how future bureaucrats and regulators choose to interpret the term "preventive care," which must be covered by all private insurance plans under the new law. If they define it to include abortion, then every insurance plan in the nation would have to cover it.

In short, the passage of Obamacare represents a significant shift toward taxpayer underwriting of abortions.

MISSED OPPORTUNITIES: TWO REAL REFORM MEASURES THAT WERE IGNORED

Almost as appalling as all the unnecessary damage done by the crafters of Obamacare is the fact that it utterly refused to do a couple of positive things that would have actually made things better for everyone.

The first and most obvious was to address the cancerous, debilitating problem of the medical liability system. The second was fixing the deeply flawed Medicare physician reimbursement formula. Nevertheless, as our nation's health care system was being remade, the folks running the show in Washington, D.C. resolutely refused to fix either one.

On the lack of reform of our medical justice system, already it has been suggested that the close affinity of the Democratic Party, the American Trial Lawyers Association, and their political benevolence may play a role. But also consider this: remember Zeke Emanuel's admonition to doctors to "relax and enjoy it"? Some doctors are leaving their practices and being absorbed by hospitals and health plans because it provides them refuge from large medical liability premiums that they have been paying in private practice. If they are absorbed by a hospital, an academic medical center, or a community health center, they are now covered by an institutional policy, and that large entry on the Accounts Payable part of the ledger goes away. Why fix the medical justice system when it is driving so many doctors out of private practice into the waiting arms of Brother Zeke's integrated delivery system of the future?

More to come in the next chapter as I reveal some things I suspect your doctor wishes his or her patients understood a little better. And I will take these subjects up in Chapter 12 as I write out a prescription for real and meaningful health care reform.

CHAPTER ELEVEN

SEVEN THINGS YOUR DOCTOR WISHES YOU KNEW

THE JULY 2010 ISSUE OF *READER'S DIGEST* OFFERED AN ARTICLE WITH A tantalizing title: "41 Secrets Your Doctor Would Never Share."[69] The piece was based on candid submissions from twenty-four physicians representing a variety of specialties and practice types. Some spoke anonymously but others allowed their names to be attached to their quotes. All spoke freely.

The secrets revealed ranged from the profound to the silly. One doc mentioned that it annoys him when patients leave their cell phones on during consultations. One mentioned she feels insulted when patients assume she is a nurse just because is a woman. Perhaps more disturbing was the admonition, "Plan for a time when bulk of your medical care will come from less committed doctors willing to work for much lower wages. Plan for a very impersonal and rushed visit during which the true nature of the problems will likely never be addressed and issues just under the surface will never be uncovered."[70]

The *Reader's Digest* article provides an interesting, if somewhat random glimpse into the world doctors inhabit. The fact remains that there are some other important, little-known realities about your doctor and his practice. And I suspect your physician has no interest in keeping them a secret. He or she may be reluctant to burden or bore you with them, but they are most likely very much on his or her mind every time you visit his or her office. Here are seven for your consideration.

1. Your doctor's practice is drowning in a rising tide of paperwork.
One study published in 2010 revealed that the documentation burden heaped upon new residents is now twice what it was twenty years ago.[71] Researchers at the Mayo Clinic found that a majority of residents reported spending as many as six hours a day documenting, while only a small fraction of residents spent as much time with patients.

As it turns out, this is a sadly apropos introduction for young doctors into the world of primary care. Recent academic studies had revealed that paperwork accounts for about a third of the typical primary care physician's workday. Similar studies reveal that primary care docs are only able to spend between eight and seventeen minutes with each patient and carry an annual load of around 3,000 patients.[72]

In other words, if your doctor is having trouble "seeing" you, it may be that he is in the middle of a "white out" blizzard of paper. Feeding this storm are the demands associated with the varied requirements of dozens of insurance companies, HMOs, and PPOs in addition to an increasingly complex matrix of requirements associated with Federal reimbursement programs like Medicare. All of this in order to, hopefully, eventually, get paid. By the way, the amount they get paid is frequently either frozen or shrinking in the face of rising costs.

For men and women who almost certainly entered the medical field because they wanted to spend their days practicing the healing arts on patients, those realities are quite demoralizing. And that demoralization is driving trends on two ends of the physician career continuum. On one end, too few of our brightest students choose medicine as a career and those who do increasingly choose salaried positions in large corporate groups rather than assuming the risks associated with owning a practice. On the other end, many of our most experienced doctors are contemplating getting out of medicine altogether.

Little in the Patient Protection and Affordable Care Act passed in 2010 holds the hope of reversing these trends. Indeed, it will surely accelerate them. An advocate of an approach called "concierge medicine" described it this way:

> If this is where healthcare is headed, we are in a lot of trouble. Family physicians who have to compete with growing paperwork, smaller gross income, and more patients, will grow too stressed . . . our physician shortage is well onto becoming a crisis sooner than we are expecting.[73]

2. Your doctor is battling to preserve the quality of your care.

As should be clear by now, there are many forces working to pull the quality of patient care downward and many factors complicating the traditional doctor-patient relationship. The encouraging news is that doctors are not going down without a fight.

For example, American physicians' net income dropped about 10 percent between 1997 and 2005. This widely reported fact prompted a study published in the *Archives of Internal Medicine* that set out to determine if doctors had begun shortening their patient visits in an effort to cram more patient visits into their days and thereby compensate for the drop in income. The surprising results of the study revealed that just the opposite had taken place. Even with paperwork burdens rising and incomes sinking due to diminishing reimbursements, the average time per doctor visit actually increased.[74]

As the published paper on the study reported: "The average visit increased from 18 to 20.8 minutes. And there was greater use of quality measures, such as medication reviews and blood pressure screenings."[75]

These findings comport with what I observed across three decades of medical practice. Doctors care about their patients. The prospect of helping people get better and live better is what drew most of them to medicine in the first place. Sure, as in any profession, there are some bad apples among them. And there are good people who simply chose the career for the wrong reasons. But the overwhelming majority of them are fighting valiantly to preserve those things about our health care system that are in the best interests of both patients and those who provide their medical care.

Sadly, most primary care doctors have long found themselves caught in a no-win squeeze between insurance companies, the government, and their sworn oaths to work in the best interests of their patients. Making matters worse, there is usually one additional burden complicating this already complex equation. That brings us to our next item . . .

3. An ever-present fear of being sued overshadows much of what your doctor says and does.

In that *Reader's Digest* feature mentioned at the beginning of this chapter, an emergency room physician from Colorado Springs offered this starkly honest confession: "Not a day goes by when I don't think about the potential for being sued. It makes me give patients a lot of unnecessary tests that are potentially harmful, just so I don't miss an injury or problem that comes back to haunt me in the form of a lawsuit."[76]

I understand this doctor's fear. Late one night several years ago I was called out in the middle of the night to assist another physician with an emergency Cesarean Section. I rushed to the hospital to help, but things did not go well that evening. Sadly, the baby did not survive.

Other than assisting in a time of crisis, I had played no role in diagnosing or treating this patient throughout her pregnancy or her labor. I rendered no opinions, made no recommendations, and did not interpret any tests. I submitted no bill to the patient or their insurance carrier for payment.

I had simply responded when the call for help went out during a crisis. But two years later, I was included in a lawsuit. And not only was I named—my brother and my father were also. Their only involvement was to share my last name, professional degree, and a position on the hospital staff. Months later we were all subsequently released from the lawsuit, but only after all of our insurance carriers had hired lawyers and filled out multiple, lengthy "discovery forms" each detailing our noninvolvement. This served as an early lesson for me in how arbitrary and unjust things can get when our medical system intersects with our legal system. Doctors are human and make mistakes. But every working doctor today is acutely aware that he or she doesn't have to make a mistake to get sued.

On average, one-doctor-in-eight is slapped with a medical liability lawsuit each year. Among the cases that ultimately go to trial, about 90 percent will be won by the doctor being sued, but only after incurring an average defense expense of around $100,000. These costs are usually born by the doc's malpractice insurer, who then must try to recoup the losses through premiums paid by doctors, who must then try to recoup the lost income. Higher losses mean higher costs for all.

Of course many cases never make it to trial. Even when the doctor has done nothing wrong, insurers often determine that settling out of court is less expensive in the long run than a lengthy jury trial. As Lawrence J. McQuillan, Director of Business and Economic Studies and a senior fellow in political economy at the Pacific Research Institute notes:

> From 1986-2002, the average insurance payment for a medical liability claim more than tripled, from $95,000 to $320,000. Yet, in 40 percent of all cases, there is no evidence of medical error or injury. The average jury award for medical liability also skyrocketed to nearly $638,000 in 2006, the most recent year for which data is available. The average settlement was about $336,000. Insurance premiums for doctors and hospitals have jumped to keep pace with increasing awards.[77]

Although the pockets of plaintiff's lawyers get filled, this abuse of the court system exacts costs that go far beyond the jury awards and rising liability insurance premiums. The hidden costs to our economy are staggering.

As the quote by the emergency room physician above illustrates, more and more doctors today at every level of the medical system feel forced to practice what has come to be called "defensive medicine"—routinely ordering unnecessary tests, referrals, and procedures purely to protect themselves against allegations of negligence. By some estimates, nearly 90 percent of primary care physicians admit to succumbing to the pressure to engage in defensive medicine.[78]

As a poll conducted by the Massachusetts Medical Society revealed, "83 percent of doctors surveyed said they have practiced so-called defensive medicine and that an average of 18 to 28 percent of tests, procedures, referrals, and consultations, and 13 percent of hospitalizations, were ordered to avoid lawsuits."[79]

What is true in the Bay State is true in all but a handful of states. By some conservative estimates, over-treatment of this type adds $191 billion to America's health care costs each year. The handful of states that are bucking this disastrous trend are those that, like my home state of Texas, have passed some form of liability reform in the form of caps on noneconomic damages.

Further evidence of this epidemic's debilitating effects came in the form of a 2009 study at New York Medical College. It revealed that fear of lawsuits was behind the increasingly common over-prescribing of antibiotics that, in turn, is driving the rise of the deadly MRSA strain of bacteria which is resistant to all but the newest antibiotics.[80]

Of course, doctors make mistakes. They're human. But a mistake is not the same thing as negligence or malpractice. Unfortunately, the current atmosphere of fear and caution engendered by fear of litigation makes doctors reluctant to admit small mistakes or make apologies, even when they genuinely want to do so.

I'm sure many physicians would echo the sentiments expressed by a doctor named James Dillard who was quoted in the *Reader's Digest* "41 Secrets" article. He said, "In many ways, doctors are held to an unrealistic standard. We are never, ever allowed to make a mistake. I don't know anybody who can live that way."[81]

4. The rewards of practicing medicine have been diminishing every year. Another compelling quote from that *Reader's Digest* piece came from a family physician in Redding, California. Dr. Vance Harris wrote: "It saddens me that my lifelong enjoyment and enthusiasm for medicine has all but died. I have watched reimbursement shrink, while overhead has more than doubled. I've been forced to take on more patients. I work 12- to 14-hour days and come in on weekends. It's still the most amazing job in the world, but I am exhausted all the time."[82]

I can't tell you how many times I have heard a good doctor repeat some form of that same lament. Of course, people of every profession and line of work grouse and grumble. It's human nature to do so. But when people who have spent hundreds of thousands of dollars getting a four-year undergraduate degree, plus four years in medical school and then several more years in internships and residencies working long hours for peanuts give serious thought to walking away, we need to pay attention.

When I first began my practice in 1981, a full day was fifteen patient visits. As time went on, the reductions in reimbursements by both Medicare and private insurance required doctors in our practice to work longer hours and see more patients per hour. Most practices have to meet a fixed overhead amount before they have anything to take home at the end of the month. When reimbursements shrunk—either because of a renegotiated contract, or a congressionally mandated Medicare fee reduction, most doctors predictably tried to increase their patient load to compensate. But there are limits to how many patients per hour one can see and how many hours per day one can work. At the end of my practice, I was scheduling thirty-five patients per day, starting one hour earlier and working one hour later just to keep up. As such my schedule was always full. If I had an emergency or someone who just simply need to be " worked in," we somehow made time to see them. But it was a very stressful way to practice medicine, not only for me, but for my staff and certainly for my patients.

It is true that doctors historically have enjoyed a comfortable standard of living, but as I often point out to my non-physician professional friends, I had the equivalent of 2 1/2 full time jobs. There was a full work week seeing patients in the office, a second forty-hour week with hospital activities such as surgeries, deliveries, and emergency room calls coupled with hospital rounds and consultations. After all that I usually averaged another twenty hours per week managing the business aspects of my practice: trying to keep up with insurance companies, making certain that capital needs were met, and making plans for expansion in the future.

When Athena Health and Sermo commissioned a survey of physicians on the eve of passage of Obamacare, they found a shocking percentage of physicians contemplating leaving the practice of medicine. They also found a full 79 percent said they are "less optimistic about the future of medicine." A full two-thirds reported considering dropping out of government health programs such as Medicare. And more than half were considering opting out of all insurance—essentially moving to a cash-only basis.[83]

Similar research has been conducted by the Physicians' Foundation, with equally troubling results. In 2008, they surveyed more than 12,000 physicians across the nation making it one of the most ambitious polls of doctors ever undertaken. According to the non-profit group, "The results paint a grim picture that could have drastic implications for the nation's health care debate."[84] Among the results:

- An overwhelming majority of physicians—78 percent—believe there is a shortage of primary care doctors in the United States today.
- 49 percent of physicians—more than 150,000 doctors nationwide—said that over the next three years they plan to reduce the number of patients they see or stop practicing entirely.
- 94 percent said the time they devote to non-clinical paperwork in the last three years has increased, and 63 percent said that the same paperwork has caused them to spend less time per patient.
- 82 percent of doctors said their practices would be "unsustainable" if proposed cuts to Medicare reimbursement were made.
- 60 percent of doctors would not recommend medicine as a career to young people.[85]

Barack Obama ran for the presidency on a platform of hope and change. With the passage of Obamacare, an already demoralized and frustrated corps of primary care doctors got even more pessimistic. That may be *change*, but doctors are rapidly losing *hope*.

5. Something magic happens when you spend your own money.
The one overriding concern from the summer of 2009 was the ever-increasing cost of healthcare. The one metric that was consistently applied was: does the proposed reform do anything to control costs in the system?

The answer then and the answer now is an emphatic "NO!" In fact, quite the opposite is true. Seven months after passage of this new law, as companies and individuals begin to renew their insurance policies, they are hit with sticker shock, with some reports of eye-popping increases in premiums in the first year of Obamacare.

So this begs the question, was it possible to do anything to control costs? A couple of quick points. When we talk about the increase in federal spending, it is the part that is already baked into the cake—entitlements and mandatory spending—that is the real accelerant to the growth of federal spending. The demographics of the Medicare-age population are rapidly growing, and the long-term care obligations from Medicaid are continually increasing. Under Obamacare, if the government's role in providing health care increases after establishment of subsidies in the exchanges, as is planned beginning in 2014, the cost will rise even more.

So how to slow the growth, or "bend the cost curve" ?

Do we ration?

Do we create waiting lists?

Do we cap the amount of care that any one patient may receive?

Do we make yet further and deeper cuts to doctors and hospitals?

In fact all the above are included in this new health reform law. But what if instead you put people in charge of their own money when it comes to making health care decisions?

Recently Republican Governor Mitch Daniels from Indiana addressed a forum at the Congressional Health Caucus. He described how he has been able to control costs of care for the coverage of state employees in Indiana with his "Healthy Indiana" program.[86]

The program is essentially set up as a conventional High Deductible Health Plan with a Health Savings Account. Gov. Daniels has been able to reduce costs for insuring state employees by 11 percent over the previous two years. The premiums for the high deductible health plan are less than those from a comparable conventional PPO. A portion of that saved premium is used to fund the individual employee's Health Savings Account with an amount generous enough to cover the high deductible part of the base plan. At the end of the year, money unused and remaining in a Health Savings Account remains with the employee, thus available to offset future health expenses. Over time individual accounts may become substantial. But the big news is that people became more cost-conscious when shopping for medical care if they knew they would be spending their own funds, even if those funds had originated from the state.

So rather than a government or an employer or an insurance company making decisions about whether or not a patient needs care, it is the patient and the doctor alone who make those decisions. And after all that is how medical care is supposed to work.

6. People do need to take responsibility for their own health.

The jury is in. Increasingly, our lifestyles are killing us. And contrary to the conventional governmental wisdom, the answer isn't more "awareness." Is there anyone above the age of ten in America who doesn't know smoking is highly addictive and deadly? Or that a steady, vegetable-free diet of processed foods is a prescription for obesity, diabetes, and host of other maladies? Or that having unprotected sex with multiple partners or sharing needles puts you in the fast lane to diseases for which there is currently no cure?

We know we need to exercise—if only an hour of walking every day. We know stress is at the root of a host of disorders. We know.

And yet a major segment of American society wants to ignore all of this knowledge and then have their doctor "fix it" when things begin to break down. We're not unlike an irresponsible Wall Street financial firm who plays fast and loose with high-risk investments and then, when things inevitably go wrong, get in line for a government bailout.

A British health and wellness magazine put it this way:

> Most people have excuses for poor health. "I just love my food too much;" "I know I'm overweight but I've tried to diet and it didn't work;" I am only eating 900 calories a day, there must be an hormonal imbalance- don't you have a pill for that?;" "I don't have time to exercise;" "Healthy food is boring;" "I've given up smoking several times, but I just start up again;" "I wish I could cut down how much I drink but I just don't seem to be able." These are some excuses we make to ourselves, and the loser is ... us! Most people don't take responsibility for their own health, and are therefore responsible for having poor health. If you think that your doctor or the government is responsible for your health, then it is time to think again.[87]

Or as an Emergency Room physician from Colorado Springs bluntly put it, "I wish patients would take more responsibility for their own health and stop relying on me to bail them out of their own problems."[88]

Your primary care doctor will probably be more tactful about it, but he or she does indeed care about your health. And if you're told you need to lose thirty pounds and start an exercise regimen, you will find a lot of appreciation, and probably a look of pleasant surprise on the face of your physician if you take that advice seriously and follow through.

7. The more the business side of practicing medicine becomes about "reimbursement" from government agencies, the more government reimbursement tables and schedules drive the practice of medicine.

Let's go to that *Reader's Digest* collection of "secrets" one last time. A family physician practicing in the Washington, D.C. area shares, "Doctors respond to market forces. If the reimbursement system is fee-for-service, that results in more services. If you build a new CT scan, someone will use it, even though having a procedure you don't need is never a good thing."[89]

This doctor is pointing out a harsh truth about our health care system. Doctors and hospitals, being rational creatures (for the most part), will do their best to survive by adapting to whatever conditions are imposed upon them by the government and insurance companies. And currently, both tend to only reimburse doctors for three things—patient visits, procedures, and tests. So guess what doctors are forced to focus on?

Yet running a medical practice that is both fiscally healthy and effective for patients involves so much more than those items. Much can, should be, and often is done by phone. Some things can be done by email. A typical primary care doctor's day also involves filling prescriptions, reviewing imaging reports and lab results, and of course, managing lots of paperwork. Robert Wachler, MD, points out why this reality is incompatible with the current reimbursement paradigm:

> This wouldn't be such a big deal if—like attorneys—primary care doctors billed out their time in six-minute aliquots, or by activity. But PCPs aren't paid that way—the office visit is ostensibly the only billable event in the life of the practice (except when they buy and use an office ultrasound or treadmill—small wonder that so many PCPs do just that). The catch-22 is obvious and tragic: the incentives drive PCPs to maximize office visits, while both patients and "the system" clearly benefit from these non-visit activities.[90]

It is tragic, indeed. Medicine is a science. But the practice of medicine, to remain viable and able to serve patients, makes it a service-oriented *business* as well. But in virtually every other service business, the proprietor can charge for all of the services he or she is actually delivering. But given the dominance of insurance (private and governmental) over the payment structure of medicine, doctors cannot.

Dr. Jay Parkinson, a pediatrician and preventive medicine specialist, wrote of the frustration this creates in an opinion piece for MedPageToday.com. "This is what happens when the business model of a doctor's practice is determined by bureaucrats in Washington with very little clue about how the practice of medicine really works," Parkinson wrote. "They've decided for doctors that we'll get paid for strictly office visits and procedures when, in fact, being a good doctor is much, much more about good communication and solid relationships than the maximum volume of patients you can see in a given day. Under today's business model of medical care, it is financially impossible for doctors to be good doctors."[91]

As with most of the other pressing problems crying for reform in medicine, the Patient Protection and Affordable Care Act failed to address this challenge.

For example, one glaring omission of Obamacare was pointed out by Daniel Palestrant, MD, the founder of Sermo.com, the online community for doctors mentioned in a previous chapter. In an opinion piece he posted prior to passage of the final bill, Dr. Palestrant points out that Obamacare "maintains the AMA's monopoly on billing codes (known as Current Procedure Terminology or CPT codes)."[92]

Reimbursement schedules are the tail wagging the dog of medical practice. And these CPT codes are that tail. They literally define how many physicians go about practicing medicine. They are a primary generator of the blizzard of paperwork I mentioned above. Dr. Palestrant pulls no punches when he writes:

> Not only do we have to maintain an extraordinary overhead of staff to submit, resubmit and document around CPT codes, the system robs the physician of any leverage we have with payors. Once we have rendered care for our patients, we must submit (and often resubmit) forms to outside parties to get paid. Make no mistake, the more complex the system, the greater the opportunity payors have to delay and/or refuse payment to physicians, not to mention manipulate those reimbursements to their own advantage, as we have seen in the recent case led by the New York Attorney General against insurance companies. Their profits grow at the expense of your cash flow.[93]

You can imagine my elation some twenty-five years ago when I discovered a billing code for phone consultations with patients after hours. My "on call" nights seemed like a constant buzzing of my beeper followed by a lengthy discussion with a patient. At last! A way to be paid for my efforts. But my rejoicing was short-lived, because although there was a code for the service, no insurance covered this expense, and all those claims were denied.

There is much more I could share but only by diving much deeper into the swamp of acronyms and regulations than any reader should be asked to go. Let it suffice to repeat what I have already suggested—that the current reimbursement-driven environment in which doctors are forced to live makes many of them long for the simpler days in which patients without the means to pay could satisfy their doctor bill with live chickens.

Put this entire list together and you begin to get a picture as to why so many in the medical community were at first encouraged by the prospect of health care reform and then profoundly disappointed at what the president and Congress ultimately produced.

Of course there is wisdom in the old saying, "Better to light a candle than to curse the darkness." Everything I have written on the preceding pages prompts a question: What would genuine, meaningful health care reform look like? Or put another way, "If you could start all over with the health care reform process, what your plan look like, Dr. Burgess?"

That's a fair question. In the following, final chapter, I'll offer a straight answer.

CHAPTER TWELVE

A PRESCRIPTION FOR WHAT'S REALLY AILING US

ONE OF THE MOST MADDENING THINGS ABOUT THE PROCESS THAT LED TO the passage of Obamacare was hearing the President and his surrogates repeatedly claim that Democrats were the only ones bringing their ideas and proposals forward about health care. In the 111th Congress, Republicans offered no fewer than thirty bills providing workable, innovative solutions and improvements to our health system. Not one of them saw the light of day in Nancy Pelosi's congress.

During the presidential campaign 2008, I was a health care surrogate for Sen. John McCain's campaign. Shortly after the November election, during a lame-duck session of Congress, I asked for a meeting with the transition team of President-elect Obama. I knew that health care would be high on their agenda because of the many nights I spent debating my counterparts on President Obama's campaign staff. But, I reasoned that I had not relinquished a twenty-five-year medical career to sit on the sidelines while someone else made all the decisions about reforming the nation's health-care system. I explained this to the President's team when they met with me. Clearly there were policies that I would not be able to support, but my feeling was that there might be some common ground that we could reach. And just maybe I could prevent something really bad from happening.

The members of the President's team thanked me for my interest, and I never heard back from them.

In July of 2009, just prior to the August recess, President Obama made a stunning offer. If any member of Congress was having trouble understanding the health care bill before the House, that member was invited to the White House to go through the bill "line by line" with the President. I jumped at the chance and immediately fired off a letter accepting the invitation. But several days later I received an indirect message that: "Dr. Burgess will not be coming to the White House."[94]

Meanwhile, the President and his spokesman Robert Gibbs took great delight in labeling Republicans "The Party of 'No'" and repeating the falsehood that we weren't bringing ideas to the table. It simply wasn't true.

At a White House briefing on April 28, 2009, press secretary Robert Gibbs said: "Well, I've said this before, I think others have said this before, that the Republican Party has to put together and put forward ideas and constructive solutions to the problems facing the people in America. The President has asked that—has asked for their help and support, but believes at the same time they have to be willing to help on the other side. And I think you heard me and others say that you can't just be the party of no or the party of no new ideas."[95]

Almost a full year later, Gibbs was still singing that same tune. On February 2, 2010, Gibbs told reporters that if the Republicans would only come up with an alternative to President Obama's plan instead of just criticizing it, he'd be happy to post it on the White House Website. Referring to the much-hyped, upcoming "health care summit" in which some Republican lawmakers were (finally) invited to discuss health care with the President, Gibbs said: "The President posted ideas of his on the White

House Website today. We hope Republicans will post their ideas either on their Website, or we'd be happy to post them on ours, so that the American people could come to one location and find out the parameters of what will largely be discussed on Thursday."

Immediately after the press briefing, a few objective reporters pointed that our detailed plan had been online for months and a link to that plan was already sitting on the White House health care Webpage. Sadly, most of the media faithfully parroted Gibbs' talking point that Republicans have no plan and no ideas. As National Review's Daniel Foster observed the next day:

> Perhaps the most widely repeated Democratic talking point in advance of tomorrow's health-care summit is that the Republicans have yet to offer an alternative plan of their own. The point is not that Republican alternatives are misguided or underdeveloped, mind you, but that they *don't exist*. By any and every measure, this is false.
>
> And yet it persists with a kind of Orwellian rigor, as if every Republican health-care proposal on offer could be "disappeared" by the brute-force insistence that they never were.[96]

Even more galling was the fact that some proposals were so detailed that they had already been scored by the CBO, meaning that the Congressional Budget Office had been able to calculate the impact on the budget and on health care premiums. The finding was that our plan would lower health care insurance premiums by 10 percent. In contrast, the Democrats plan could not be scored by the CBO because there were too many unknowns and not enough detail. There were literally "back of the envelope" calculations in circulation which passed for a "CBO score".

In the face of all this, White House Communications Director Dan Pfeiffer was at it again the very next morning with a post on the White House blog headlined, "Will the Republicans Post Their Health Plan . . . and When?"[97] It would have been comical if the results for the American people and the American economy weren't so tragically high.

In truth, there have been multiple Republican proposals—Paul Ryan of Wisconsin, Dave Camp of Michigan, and myself all had detailed plans forward.[98]

Right after the summer town halls in August of 2009, it became apparent to me that the extremely large and complicated thousand-page bill about health care seemed to upset a lot of people. My feeling was that we would do well to offer alternatives, but alternatives that were focused on existing, known problems in the system; and of course on holding down increases in the cost of health care.

The previous few chapters have been an overview of how the important work of reforming America's health care system got predictably fouled up. The story is a tragic one because the truth is, our system did (and does) need significant reform.

I was no fan of the status quo prior to Obamacare. In fact, my very decision to run for office was driven by a desire to help my country by helping repair and improve our system. Yes, it was still the best medical system in the world but some endemic and systemic problems—some caused by government interventions that were distorting the health care markets—were pushing us rapidly in the wrong direction.

I had two reforms in particular in mind as I ran for office the very first time. One involved repairing the very broken system governing Medicare reimbursements to health care givers. The other addressed a key driver behind unnecessary testing and treatment that in turn is a major reason for rising costs, i.e., fear of non-meritorious law suits. Sadly, the crafters of Obamacare not only refused to address these problems in the legislation but also refused to even acknowledge they were problems.

The vast majority of what Obamacare put in place needs to be undone. But that will still leave us with the task of accomplishing the kind of real reform that our nation needs in order to advance health care innovation, delivery and access—for all Americans. Here are nine key elements that constitute a powerful prescription for healing what's ailing us. For several of these, legislation that makes the reform a reality has already been drafted. We just a need enough citizens to demand these reforms so we can have a Congress that will pass them. (And, of course, a president who will sign them.)

Prescription 1—Insurance Reform

Health insurance has been a wonderful innovation, allowing groups of unrelated individuals to pool their risk and aggregate their buying power. But as I've pointed out previously, those underlying costs that health insurance policies must cover keep rising.

When my grandfather began practicing medicine, the most sophisticated piece of equipment a hospital might possess was an x-ray machine. Today an astonishing array of sophisticated diagnostic equipment—from open MRI, to PET scans, to bone density DEXA scanners and gene sequencers—has come online, along with new technology-driven treatments utilizing fiber optic cameras, robotics, and lasers. And more are being developed weekly.

Of course the research, development, creation, and acquisition of all this technology is expensive, as are the trained personnel to operate it, but it represents one of the reasons most of us are living longer and better. This is one of the factors driving health care costs—and therefore health insurance premiums—higher and higher. But it is far from the only factor.

Some of the other reforms we will examine offer real hope for addressing these other drivers of increasing cost. But one thing is certain, in a world in which diagnosis and treatment are increasingly expensive, it is vital that people with pre-existing conditions be able to acquire health insurance, and in a way that doesn't unfairly burden other policy holders with exorbitant premiums, push insurers into insolvency, or saddle future generations with additional mountains of government debt through yet another unsustainable entitlement program.

This is no small challenge. For people with pre-existing conditions that require ongoing and expensive care, the money to pay for that care must come from *somewhere*. Some people in Washington seem to think that our government can forever continue to issue IOUs in the form of Treasury Bonds and have the Federal Reserve print money to buy them. That's a prescription for fiscal catastrophe.

Nevertheless, there are some sensible ways to eliminate the bias against patients with pre-existing conditions. For one thing, there is a striking difference in the way people with pre-existing conditions are handled through employer-based group insurance policies and through the private policy market serving those who are not covered at work. Currently, if you are joining a group plan through work, you cannot be denied coverage because of a pre-existing condition. But if you are trying to buy health coverage on your own, you can. This needs to change.

By the way, forcing everyone to buy coverage through an individual mandate misses the point here. Insurance will become too expensive, or large segments of the population will be denied coverage because they have been ill in the past. An individual mandate coupled with guaranteed issue almost assures us that people will avoid purchasing insurance because they know it will be available to them if they truly become severely ill. Think of it this way: the desk for purchasing auto insurance is located in the new car show room, not the body shop.

Meaningful insurance reform should also narrow the circumstances under which insurance companies can rescind (cancel) policies once they are in place. We should make sure no insurance company can exploit vagueness in regulatory language in order to rescind a policy rather than pay an expensive claim. Insurance regulations should outlaw rescissions except in clear cases of fraud, and ensure that states have well-designed, high-risk pools to handle people with pre-existing conditions.

What would legislation that accomplishes these goals look like? We don't have to guess. Prior to the passage of Obamacare, former Congressman Nathan Deal (now the Governor of Georgia) and I had already authored a couple of bills that would move us well down that road. In the spring of 2009, Nathan Deal was our highest-ranking Republican on the health subcommittee of the Committee on Energy and Commerce. Nathan, multiple staff members, and I worked late into the night for several weeks trying to solve the conundrum of pre-existing conditions without an individual mandate. Since Nathan had already filed to run in Georgia's gubernatorial primary, he was particularly sensitive to not creating additional burdens or mandates for the states. HR 4019 and HR 4020 introduced in the 111th congress are products of those late-night work sessions.

Congressman Deal authored HR 4019, summarized by its title: Limiting Pre-Existing Condition Exclusions in All Health Insurance Markets. This allows a health insurer in the individual market to impose preexisting condition exclusion only to the extent that such an exclusion is already present in the group health insurance market. The intent was to provide some of the protections of the group health insurance market in the individual market. Speaker Pelosi and her allies made sure those bills never saw the light of day. A similar bill I introduced around the same time suffered a similar fate—dying in committee. My HR 4020: Guaranteed Access to Health Insurance Act would have helped accomplish something virtually every proponent of Obamacare said was an important goal: getting the majority of America's uninsured people covered by health insurance by eliminating those obstacles posed by having a "preexisting condition." This legislation provides grants to states to adopt a program for either pooling risk, or reinsurance to assist states in this endeavor. Thus risk pools and reinsurance would have a shared federal, state, and private sector contribution for patients who required such coverage. The idea was to make it affordable and available for people who were caught in a pre-existing condition conundrum. True, there was an expense associated with this; an earlier estimate by the Congressional Budget Office had placed this cost at $20 billion over ten years time. We both felt that this figure was too low and provided $25 billion in the legislation. A significant sum to be sure, but since this segment of the population was driving a great deal of the debate leading up to the passage of the President's health care law, it seemed reasonable to try to provide a solution. Of course $25 billion contained in this legislation is nowhere near the $1 trillion or more contained within the President's proposal.

Prescription 2—Tax Fairness

The above-mentioned goal of getting more Americans covered by health insurance was talked about incessantly during the debate over Obamacare. And it's a worthy goal. You will recall that oft-cited figure of 47 million uninsured individuals in America, the number I unpacked for you in Chapter 6. I pointed out how a significant portion of those individuals not covered by an employer's group policy had chosen not to purchase insurance—either because they were young and didn't feel the need for it, or found it so expensive they couldn't justify the expense.

Some public officials have long argued that we could get many more in that latter group covered through a simple change in our tax policy. Currently, people who purchase insurance privately—in other words are not part of a group plan through their place of employment—are at a tax disadvantage to those who contribute to their group health coverage at work. Changing this disparity so that individuals receive the same tax benefits no matter where they get their health insurance help would move a significant number of new people into the "insured" column. In other words, we need to offer tax credits to help individuals purchase insurance in the private market.

By now, you won't be surprised to learn that the Republicans had offered a bill that would do just that, and much, much more. I am referring to HR 3218, the Improving Health Care for All Americans Act authored by Congressman John Shadegg of Arizona.

Compared to the 1,100+ plus page paper mountain that was Obamacare, Shadegg's bill was a mere twenty-four pages long and yet offers much more in the way of real and meaningful reform. It also doesn't call for a single additional penny of additional federal spending whereas the legislation that passed is estimated to carry a $1.4 trillion price tag.

There were three key elements in Shadegg's bill. This trio of reforms, along with legal liability reform, makes up a sensible, workable core of an effort to fix what is broken with our health care system without breaking other things that we should all want to preserve.

They are: (1) Refundable tax credits for medical costs;

(2) Expansion of access to health insurance coverage through individual membership associations; and

(3) Incentivizing the creation of high risk pools.

Allow me to give you a brief overview of each of these ideas.

Refundable Tax Credits—Under HR 3218, any one taxpayer who pays for health care insurance would see a tax credit equal to the amount they paid toward premiums and any out-of-pocket medical care costs for the entire year (with a cap of $2,500 if filing individually or $5,000 if filing jointly.)

Please note we're talking about a tax credit for money spent, not an income tax deduction. This is better. Up to $5,000 comes right off of the household's tax bill or is added to any refund. Thus this credit would not be extended to those who receive medical care reimbursements through Medicare, Social Security, or other government programs.

Expanding Access to Health Insurance—One of the more innovative aspects of HR 3218 is that it allows various legal entities such as churches, schools, and other types of organizations to offer health insurance coverage to its members. One of the biggest challenges for entrepreneurs and other self-employed people is that group health insurance is so much more affordable and easier to obtain than individual policies, yet these and others often don't have access to group policies. This provision should significantly increase the quantity and availability of group insurance.

This feature would allow social service organizations, such as charities, to provide health insurance coverage to the poor or to the mentally ill. Think about it. America's homelessness problem is very much linked to the scourges of mental illness and addiction. How much homelessness could be eliminated if enterprising social services agencies, backed by compassionate donors, could provide the health insurance that could enable many people to be free of these root causes?

High Risk Pools—Finally, the Shadegg legislation proposed that the federal government match 50 cents for every dollar that individual states lay out to create and fund high-risk insurance pools—the kind necessary to enable the insuring of folks with pre-existing conditions. More than thirty states already operate such pools.

High risk pools offer the coverage very much like that of traditional policies, but with one major distinction. These can be customized for a variety of chronic illnesses and provide benefits specific to those particular illnesses. Like conventional policies, they can be purchased in the form of HMOs, PPOs, or indemnity plans.

Prescription 3—Medical Liability Reform

Abuse of the medical justice system is rampant, debilitating, and costly. Yes, such abuse is driving malpractice insurance premiums up to the point at which many doctors are considering leaving the practice of medicine, particularly in specialties such as obstetrics. But it is doing much more. It is a key factor in the rampant rise in the cost of medicine as fear of being sued leads practitioners at every level to order expensive tests and treatments.

Cost estimates are difficult to ascertain, but consider just the cost of liability insurance in the five years before I left active practice. Liability rates more than doubled from $25,000 in 1997 to $53,000 in 2002. Then, in 2003, Texas undertook major medical liability reform by capping non-economic damages.

In any liability claim there are recovered costs for actual damages: the cost of care, the cost of lost wages, and loss of earning potential. But there are also recoveries for so-called "noneconomic" damages. Pain and suffering, loss of companionship, and other intangibles fall into this category.

The problem with noneconomic damages is that they are harder to quantify, the amounts awarded can be subject to wide interpretation. As a consequence these damages add significant uncertainty to the liability equation because of the unpredictability of these amounts. Some states have provided an upper limit on noneconomic damages: California enacted a $250,000.00 cap in 1975 and Texas enacted a $750,000.00 cap in 2003. Both of these were an attempt to bring stability to the pricing of jury awards. After the cap, Texas, which had been in a "liability crisis," saw a normalization of insurance rates.

Liability insurance rates for an obstetrician/gynecologist in Dallas-Fort Worth fell to $37,000 in 2008. Clearly, this reform made a significant difference upon liability rates in Texas, but more importantly, it allowed physicians to return to the state or their practice.

When I was in Nome, Alaska, for a Chamber of Commerce function, a group of doctors came up to me and voiced excitement that Congress might pass a federal cap on noneconomic damages. They told me that they were eager for liability reform to pass, and soon. Because of high liability insurance rates, their hospital could not afford to employ an anesthesiologist.

I asked one doctor what type of practice he had, and he said, "Just like you, I'm an obstetrician." I asked him how he was practicing obstetrics without an anesthesiologist on staff, and he admitted that this was very difficult. Not only were they unable to offer epidural anesthesia during labor, but if a patient required a C-section, it required an emergency evacuation to an Anchorage hospital. Because of the distances involved, this frequently means an air-evacuation. And it is my understanding that weather conditions in Nome Alaska are frequently bad. How can it possibly be in the interest of patients and patient care to allow such a broken system to continue unaddressed?

So serious is this problem that some states have indeed tackled it by passing liability reform at the state level. My home state of Texas is one of them and the results have been most encouraging.

A perinatologist I met in 2003 recently had completed medical school, residency and fellowship, sub-specializing in the care of complicated pregnancies. Because this was deemed such a high-risk specialty, no insurance company in Dallas-Fort Worth would cover him.

Unwilling to practice without insurance coverage and risk his financial future, he started work as a computer analyst instead of caring for high-risk pregnancies. After the Texas liability reform in 2003, he obtained coverage and launched a medical practice that continues today. And I do not doubt that the mothers and their infants in the Dallas area are significantly better off because he has.

On several occasions prior to the passage of his health care reform bill, I communicated to President Obama that Texas' capping of noneconomic damages has been a success. It has improved the climate for doctors in Texas, luring more to the state, especially in medically underserved areas. Furthermore, the kind of reform Texas adopted does not deny patients who have been legitimately harmed what is due them. More importantly, Texas counties that had been without the services of an emergency room physician or an obstetrician now have that access thanks to liability reform. Fortunately for patients, some states have begun to fix their problems.

Idaho, for example, has established a pretrial hearing panel to review pending lawsuits. This panel weeds out the kinds of non-meritorious claims that chronically infest court dockets as well as facilitate the resolution of valid disputes without expensive trials. This screening process saves the taxpayers money and ultimately lowers liability insurance premiums by ensuring that judges and juries hear only cases with genuine merit.

Doctor shortages will soon be widespread and severe. But right now the severity varies widely from state to state. Why? An insightful opinion piece in the *Orange County Register* provides the explanation:

> When insurance premiums become too burdensome, physicians retire or move to states with more balanced legal climates. In some cases, patients are left with no access to local care. To prevent this outcome, some states, such as California, limit noneconomic-damage awards or punitive awards. This helps retain the physicians they have and attract new ones.
>
> Caps also lower health care costs. Research from Stanford University professor Daniel P. Kessler and Brookings Institution scholar Mark McClellan shows that caps and other reforms can lower medical expenditures by 5 percent to 9 percent without adverse effects on patients.[99]

In spite of this, and the nearly unanimous calls from the medical industry for liability reform to be included in any bundle of health care reforms, our cries fell on deaf ears. Why? Perhaps it is because the Trial Lawyers Association is one of the most powerful and well-funded lobbies in the nation. And it is a special interest group that gives an overwhelming percentage of its political support and donations to Democrats.[100] Lawyers specializing in suing doctors and hospitals have amassed astonishing fortunes. And even more staggering sums are being harvested by firms who launch class action lawsuits against the drug companies and makers of medical devices. The costs of these suits and the judgments (or more often settlements) they produce must ultimately be born by the consumers of health care.

There are other strategies for lowering liability costs, and these should be explored. But we should not sacrifice what is clearly a working and winning strategy while we look at other options. The Texas reform has worked well, and we should do no less for the people of the United States. We need national, across-the-board change in the tort reform system.

A bill I introduced in 2009 would have brought Texas-style relief to the entire system. In the "Medical Justice Act" I proposed to regulate civil actions for an injury or death resulting from health care by, among other things, limiting the noneconomic damages that an individual could recover. Doing so would go a long way toward diminishing the need for physicians to practice defensive medicine due to the fear of being second-guessed by trial lawyers.

Of that bill, Texas Medical Association president Josie R. Williams, MD said, "All Americans deserve to enjoy the benefits Texas has seen thanks to the eradication of our epidemic of health care lawsuit abuse. Since our new law took effect, Texas has licensed 14,000 new physicians, including a record 3,621 in fiscal year 2008. This has been good medicine for the people of Texas, and Dr. Burgess' plan would apply this life-saving treatment to the rest of the country."

What America got instead in Obamacare was a meaningless little token nod toward liability reform in the form of funding for some "trial studies." We can do better. States like Texas already are.

Prescription 4—Portability

Consider this. A couple of years ago the average health insurance premium for a family of four in New Jersey was $10,000. In Pennsylvania that policy cost $6,000. And in Texas, essentially identical coverage cost only $5,000. The problem for families in New Jersey is that, due to state-by-state restrictions on portability, acquiring that Texas policy isn't an option for them. So they are stuck paying twice as much.

Another problem is that, as people change jobs or move across state lines, they currently must change insurance plans. And given the frequency with which people tend to move these days, it means a significant amount of turnover or "churn" within risk pools. This gives insurance companies very little incentive to help policy holders with preventive care and early detection. A person with an unhealthy lifestyle or an undetected disease is likely to become some other insurance company's problem anyway.

I refer to this as the "NFL paradox." If a player for a football team within the National Football League is traded to a new team, his insurance policy travels with him. There is no waiting period; there is no danger of a pre-existing condition exclusion interfering with his coverage.

However, if the number one fan of this player moves to that new city his or her situation is quite different. In all likelihood their insurance policy will not be available in their new city, at least not right away. He may have to wait a period of time before he can be covered by his new insurance and if there were a pre-existing condition this individual may now find it difficult to obtain insurance at all. So how is it rational to have two versions of reality, one for the star ballplayer and another for the average fan?

Meaningful health care reform should make it possible for patients to shop for health insurance plans across state lines and also "own" their own policy, taking it with them when they move. Such "portability" would mean more choices and lower costs for consumers, not to mention more long-term predictability in risk pools for insurers.

This is a reform my colleague John Shadegg tried to bring to pass way back in 2005 when he introduced HR 2355, the "Health Care Choice Act." The Republicans still held a slim majority in the House back then. As a result, this bill actually made it out of committee, being voted on to the full house along pretty much a party line vote. But it died there without ever receiving an up or down vote. He has twice reintroduced the bill in the years since then, with similar results.

It is interesting to note who, among all the interested parties, tends to support and oppose this measure.

Insurance companies as a group were supportive. It's not hard to understand why. Currently a national health insurer must tailor up to fifty different versions of a policy to conform to the varying regulations established by each state and enforced by fifty different state insurance commissioners. Those companies could slash administrative costs if the states could be encouraged to consolidate and unify their rules and regulations.

Who opposes portability? Most vocal in opposition were those fifty state insurance commissioners who understandably saw in the bill a significant diminishment of their powers. For example, in our committee hearings on the bill, we heard two witnesses speak in opposition to the bill. One of them was the insurance commissioner for the state of Washington speaking on behalf of National Association of Insurance Commissioners.

Most conservatives, myself included, are ordinarily arguing on the side of defending state's rights and prerogatives against top-down intrusion from Washington, D.C.. But in the case of the increasingly complex and expensive realm of insurance law, a more unified national approach seems to be just the kind of thing the framers of the Constitution had in mind when they inserted the Commerce Clause, giving Congress the right to regulate interstate commerce. In fact this very type of flexibility is already available to large multistate companies. Why not have the same consideration for the "little guy"? That is why I have enthusiastically supported Rep. Shadegg's legislation every time it has been introduced.

Encouraging portability of health insurance policies and lowering the walls between states where shopping for those policies is concerned is a reform in which everyone wins (with the possible exception of those who make a living maintaining those walls.)

Prescription 5—Medicare Payment Reform
In June of 2010, an article in *USA Today* revealed what many of us have been shouting from the rooftops for years. Namely, that a growing number of medical practices were being forced by simple economics to limit the number of Medicare patients they could accept, or to stop accepting them altogether. The piece began by announcing: "The number of doctors refusing new Medicare patients because of low government payment rates is setting a new high, just six months before millions of Baby Boomers begin enrolling in the government health care program."[101]

Anyone with a reasonably open mind could see this crisis coming from miles away. While all the costs associated with running a medical practice have risen, Medicare reimbursements remained static. This has been the worst year ever for doctors seeing Medicare patients. In March 2010, Congress failed to address the looming cuts in reimbursement prior to going on its regularly scheduled Easter recess. As a result, the Center for Medicare and Medicaid Services "held" checks to keep cuts from going into effect, hoping that Congress would take up and extend current rates upon its return in mid-April. By law that period of time the checks are held cannot be for longer than fourteen days. That deadline was certainly pushed before Congress acted and took up a "Doc fix extension." But Congress only fixed the problem for sixty days, and the same thing happened again in June. Another deadline missed, another congressional recess, and again the administrator at CMS held checks for over two weeks. Congress returned and narrowly averted another disaster by passing the extension.

Or was the disaster averted? What is the effect of "holding" checks for two weeks on a small practice? Even if the number of Medicare patients within that practice is relatively small—10 or 15 percent—most medical offices are so close to the margin every month that a 10 to 15 percent reduction in cash flow is nearly catastrophic. That means no paycheck for the doctor. That may mean a short term note from the local bank to cover fixed expenses. Longer-term, it results in an inability to plan for the future. Is it any wonder that doctors look at this situation and say, "I quit"?

Compounding the tragedy is that this was all so unnecessary and preventable. Reworking the Medicare reimbursement schedule, widely called the "doc fix" for short, has been an obvious need for years. Medicare's reimbursements for services have been lower than the "market value." Those reimbursements remained stuck at artificially low levels while back-end costs for doctors continued to rise. This has only been sustainable because most medical practices had enough non-Medicare patients to compensate for any losses incurred by treating Medicare patients. But with the Baby Boomer generation reaching the Medicare threshold age of sixty-five, practices are finding themselves with Medicare patients making up an ever-larger percentage of their practice. The only way for a practice to stop that bleeding is to announce that it can accept no new Medicare patients. And that is precisely what we are seeing at an accelerating rate.

Here are three bits of supporting data from that *USA Today* article:

- The American Academy of Family Physicians says 13% of respondents didn't participate in Medicare last year, up from 8% in 2008 and 6% in 2004.
- The American Osteopathic Association says 15% of its members don't participate in Medicare and 19% don't accept new Medicare patients. If the cut is not reversed, it says, the numbers will double.
- The American Medical Association says 17% of more than 9,000 doctors surveyed restrict the number of Medicare patients in their practice. Among primary care physicians, the rate is 31%.[102]

How will this affect America's swelling ranks of Medicare patients? As columnist Ed Morrisey put it in a June 2010 online opinion piece:

It means longer wait times, much less choice, and probably a lower quality of care overall as the number of providers narrow to high-volume, low-cost clinics. Even those providers who continue to accept Medicare patients will get overwhelmed by the demand and instead of seeing doctors, patients will have to make do with triage nurses and physician's assistants. The one program that succeeded in ameliorating this process by introducing a private/public partnership, Medicare Advantage, will be emasculated over the next couple of years by massive cuts to the program.[103]

As Morrisey suggests with his reference to cuts in the Medicare Advantage program, Obamacare only serves to make all of these problems worse. So, what is the solution to this growing crisis? At the risk of sounding like a broken record, I introduced "doc fix" legislation in 2009. My "Ensuring the Future Physician Workforce Act" (HR 3693) would have tackled the Medicare reimbursement issue head on and provided a permanent fix that ensured seniors would continue to have access to their doctors.

It was a desperately needed measure when I introduced it then. It is even more urgently needed now.

Prescription 6—Create Products People Want

By passing a law with an individual mandate to buy health insurance, we have taken all of the incentive away from insurance companies to be imaginative about what their policies and products look like.

When Henry Ford first started making the Model-T, he famously announced, "You can get one in any color you want, as long as it's black." Of course people wanted colors other than black and before long cars were rolling off assembly lines in a rainbow of colors. That is the wonderful thing about free and open market. Those who provide what people want thrive and those who don't perish.

But for decades the health insurance market has been very heavily regulated. The power of markets to deliver what people are asking for has been buried under an avalanche of federal mandates and the freedom to innovate and experiment has been choked out in a dense jungle of state regulations. As a result, consumers are offered only what government tells insurers they must offer. The results have been predictable.

One of Obamacare's big selling points offers us a prime example. A key rationale for the Patient Protection and Affordable Care Act was the need to offer affordable insurance to Americans with pre-existing conditions. This is certainly an important challenge as several of my previous prescriptions have noted.

Thus we were told that Obamacare must be passed and passed quickly because hundreds of thousands of uninsured people with pre-existing conditions were waiting for an opportunity to purchase coverage. The legislation called for the Department of Health and Human Services to build an insurance policy specifically for such people and build a national risk pool around the participants.

A *Wall Street Journal* editorial on November 12, 2010 described the urgency with which the plan was sold in these terms:

> To judge by President Obama's rhetoric, the insurance industry's victims have been wandering the country like Okies in "The Grapes of Wrath." Thus Obamacare gave the Health and Human Services Department the power to design and sell its own insurance policies. The $5 billion program started in July and runs through 2014, when Obamacare's broader regulations kick in.[104]

The Obama administration anticipated adding more than 375,000 policyholders to the pool in the first year of the program. But as the editorial points out, there wasn't exactly a stampede of people rushing to buy the government's new creation. In fact, four months after the launch of the new policy, slightly more than 8,000 people had signed up. Of course, participation in the program could pick up over time, but the early indicators are that people aren't buying what the government is selling.

Perhaps the most damaging aspect of Obamacare is the individual mandate. Mandates have no place in a free society. There are some brilliant minds in the insurance industry. It would be fascinating to see what innovations those minds could come up with in the way of meeting consumer demand if given an opportunity to compete.

Health Savings Accounts are one option that offers Americans not covered by a company group policy amazing flexibility and control of their health care spending. I would love to see us challenge the insurance industry to develop similar products for other niche groups and then get out of their way long enough to let them do it. And certainly Governor Daniels of Indiana has shown the power of consumer-oriented health care in his state.

Prescription 7—Price Transparency

Imagine sitting down at a fancy new restaurant and discovering no prices on the menu. Wouldn't you be nervous about ordering—having no idea what kind of bill you were going to be socked with at the end of the meal?

Yet that is precisely how we ask people to consume medical services. When you or a loved one are in the hospital, wouldn't it be nice to know how much you're being asked to spend before you to consent to an exam or test or procedure? I think so. Let's have the prices up-front, just like in a restaurant or clothing store.

And it seems as if the answer to the question: "How much does this cost?" can be maddening. "It depends upon who is paying" is a frequent response. When I was in practice, if I recommended a test or a treatment for a patient, the next question very likely was not: "Doctor, is this necessary?" or "Doctor, is there a lower-cost option?" The next question invariably was, "Is this covered by my insurance?" If the answer to that question was yes, there was remarkably little curiosity about anything else.

That is why I authored "The Health Care Price Transparency Promotion Act" a few years ago. The bill would have directed states to establish and maintain laws requiring disclosure of information on hospital charges. Additionally, the legislation would have required hospitals and health plans to make such information available to the public, and to provide individuals with information about estimated out-of-pocket costs for health care services.

Real, meaningful reform of our health care system would certainly make consumers of health care services better informed and more empowered to make good choices. This leads naturally to my next prescription.

Prescription 8—Preventative Care and Wellness Programs

Amid the contentious, often partisan debate over health care, there are a couple of things about which there is almost universal agreement. One is that health care costs have been rising dramatically year after year. As a nation we have been spending an ever-increasing percentage of our GDP on health care. The other point of agreement is that wellness and disease prevention are keys to stopping that upward cost spiral.

The costs of preventable disease and lifestyle-related illness to the U.S. economy are staggering—running into the hundreds of billions of dollars. In 2004, in the United States, this cost employers $1,685 per employee per year, amounting to a total annual loss of $225.8 billion. It has risen dramatically and steadily in the years since. According to Dr. Pawel Suwinski, a consultant to major corporations on managing employee health care costs, at least 50 percent of medical costs are preventable by lifestyle adjustments, and 75 percent of all medical costs caused by chronic diseases are best prevented and treated by lifestyle adjustments.[105]

That means we all have a part to play in health care reform. The answer isn't making the federal government a universal nanny who scolds, cajoles, and punishes us all into living healthier lifestyles. Few folks outside of San Francisco believe that the city's recent ban on putting toys in "Happy Meals" or other fast food kid's meals will make a significant difference in the childhood obesity problem there, and rules passed down by the federal government will probably not have a massive effect either.

Nevertheless, there are ways we can release insurance companies from restrictive regulations and allow them to reward healthy lifestyle choices. With a little freedom and encouragement, insurers can provide premium rebates and other incentives to people who make healthy choices or participate in management of their chronic diseases.

This is an area in which we have a real opportunity to, in the words of President Obama, "bend the cost curve downward." So far, the health care reforms put in place in 2010 under the PPACA have done just the opposite.

Prescription 9—Doctors to Care for America's Patients

In April of 2010, the AMA estimated that one in four Medicare patients who are seeking a new primary care physician are experiencing difficulty finding one.[106]

I have referred to our current and growing doctor shortage repeatedly on the preceding pages. I have also made clear my belief that it would be unconscionable to exacerbate this shortage through bad policies (such as those which fill the Patient Protection and Affordable Care Act) and then attempt to remedy it by luring medical talent from developing nations.

Even before Obamacare, a future crisis was being driven by the simple reality that not enough bright young minds were choosing medicine as a career to replace those silver haired docs retiring each year. We should ask ourselves why.

The answer lies in the problems I have already identified in this chapter. When a gifted and ambitious young college student considers a career in medicine, he or she weighs the costs (in time, preparation, expense) against the potential rewards. Under the current system, fewer and fewer of our best and brightest conclude that the equation makes sense.

Dr. Atul Grover, chief advocacy officer for the Association of American Medical Colleges (AAMC), told the *Los Angeles Times* in June of 2010, "This will be the first time since the 1930s that the ratio of physicians to the population will start to decline. The number of people over sixty-five will double between 2000 and 2030, and the amount of medical services they require is two to three times higher than many other adults."[107]

This is already a problem in many places. Yet, the current health care legislation intend to dump another 30-to-40 million additional people into the lines forming to see a shrinking pool of doctors—and do so without addressing the root causes of the doctor shortage.

The AAMC has forecast a deficit of up to 125,000 doctors by the year 2025. This can only mean longer wait times and longer travel distances for many, especially those living in rural areas. This shortage will be especially acute among primary care physicians where people will find visits with an actual doctor rarer, briefer, and more expensive.

We must ensure that we have enough doctors to care for all of America's patients—now and in the future. That's why I have repeatedly introduced a measure I called the "Physician Workforce Enhancement Act." This law targets the weakest spots of the medical workforce: specializations like emergency medicine, obstetrics and gynecology, and pediatrics, as well as rural health programs for small and developing communities. The bill would help small hospitals that serve rural or growing areas by providing them with interest-free loans to establish a residency training program for high need medical specialties.

There you have it. A nine-point prescription that, taken together, would have a profound and positive effect on our nation's health care system. The great news is that these reforms don't need to be accomplished in one step through some complex, multi-thousand page piece of "comprehensive" legislation. Indeed, they shouldn't be. We can take on this challenge a piece at a time and in a process that is open, understandable, and gives all the affected parties an opportunity to be heard—especially the party called the American people.

Of course, we have a lot of work to do to make this a reality. But I am encouraged. The election of 2010 brought a fresh wave of doctors to Congress. Six physicians, three nurses, and one dentist will join me and the other nine doctors returning to service in the 112th Congress. And that is just on the Republican side of the aisle. I'm so pleased these men and women heard and answered their own version of a "house call."

I look forward to working with them to build national health care policies that work for patients and providers. If we're successful, and I believe we will be, perhaps one of my grandchildren will choose a career in medicine, and carry on our proud family tradition.

EPILOGUE

IN JULY 2010, SOME FOUR MONTHS AFTER PASSAGE OF PRESIDENT OBAMA'S NEW health care law, I met with a group of perhaps a dozen medical students and residents. Each had been involved over the summer in an internship or health care fellowship in Washington DC. I wanted to give them a chance to question a fellow physician who had been involved in the trenches during the health care debate that had recently ended.

One young medical student looked at me and said, "I'll bet if you had it all to do over again now, you would not go into medicine."

I replied without hesitation "I would give anything to be your age again and just starting a career in medicine today. You will have more tools at your disposal for diagnosing, treating alleviating suffering, and returning to productivity then mankind has ever known. You all will truly practice in what will be known as the Golden age of medicine. The science is progressing at such a rapid rate, new technologies and tools are being developed at an astounding pace, and the predictive value of knowing someone's genomic sequence is simply going to be a part of your world, and it will be a world unlike any previous generation of physicians has witnessed."

"Now there is no question that The Congress has screwed things up for you mightily on the policy front," I continued, "but you are all bright guys and you will be able to correct our mistakes. But while the policy may be flawed, the science is going to be spectacular. And I trust will find a way to figure it all out".

And I truly believe that. The bright young men and women that make up tomorrow's American medical contingent are going to work in a world unlike any their predecessors ever imagined. It is for that reason I feel so strongly about telling my story of how we got here, this flawed health care policy, and what I believe we must do to reverse it.

Though it presents sizable challenges, the future is exciting to contemplate. As lawmakers and citizens, we are compelled to help, not handicap, the doctors of the future, and to give them and all Americans a fair working healthcare system, worthy of the great nation in which we live.

ACKNOWLEDGMENTS

THE HAZARD INHERENT IN PROVIDING ANY LIST OF ACKNOWLEDGMENTS is that I am invariably going to leave out a large number of people who should be included. So let me begin by apologizing to that cohort of worthy acquaintances I have not mentioned because of space and the failings of memory.

But clearly the most important person who must lead this list is my wife of thirty-seven years, Laura. The many twists and turns that life has taken were not always planned, but through it all we have stayed together and are better for it. Certainly our children Christine, Jessica, and Mike have also played a very important role in the development of this book. Of course I need to thank my mother and father, who are no longer with us, for providing me a firm foundation that has allowed me the opportunity to have such vast experiences. My brother Rick, my sister Terri, and their extended families are also an important part of this endeavor.

Those that helped shape my early education, Richard Gilliard, and Roger Grote at the Selwyn School, as well as David Redden and Roland Vela at North Texas State University provided a solid educational foundation. The late Dr. Jack Pritchard and Norman (stormin' Norman) Gant at Parkland Hospital provided me experiences during my residency that could likely never be duplicated. I was fortunate to have a large number of fellow residents during my tenure who seemed to always have my back. Of that cadre of residents, Dr. George Wendell endures to this day as the head of the residency program at Parkland, and he is a frequent source of advice and information, and for that I am grateful. John McCracken at UT Dallas tried to provide management expertise.

From the time I was in medical practice, I always used to say that the world is heavily populated with my former partners, and for that reason it is impossible to name all of them. But my doctors at OB/Gyn Associates of Lewisville deserve special recognition. Dr. Leslie Auers, Dr. Bradley Axline, Dr. Vicki Allen, Dr. Andrea Galusha, and the late Dr. Gary Rose not only had confidence to work with me in a medical setting, but they also allowed me the freedom to test the political waters when I felt it was necessary to do so. I don't think any one of them thought that I would actually be successful, but they were too kind to say so initially, and then were very supportive as my campaign gathered momentum. Patty Turner who was our business manager, and continues in that role today, was skeptical but supportive as I began my political activities. My office assistants, Lori Rudolph and Martha Cody, were enormous help in balancing my practice responsibilities and my fledgling career in public service. And certainly I am grateful to Ray Dunning who was the hospital administrator at the Medical Center of Lewisville and constantly kept me apprised of the difficulty in managing a large healthcare institution.

From a political standpoint, State Sen. Jane Nelson and State Rep. Myra Crownover provided valuable early direction and advice after I identified myself as a candidate for office. Kim Ross with the Texas Medical Association and Brian Epstein also helped fulfill that role. My speech therapist, Merrie Spaeth, provided me with invaluable help in learning how to communicate to more than one person that time. Brenda Holland, the administrator at the Denton County Medical Society, was a significant help in my first campaign. And finally Kim Garza has made each episode of reelection appear effortless, and of course always successful.

I've been very fortunate to be surrounded by great staff in both my Washington DC office in my district offices back home. I am always mindful, however, as Gov. Mitch Daniels warned me that in the Bible, Isaac died while leaning on his staff, so I try not to make their life too difficult. My Chief of Staff in Washington has not changed from the first day I was sworn in. Barry Brown has provided capable leadership and seems to show no signs of wearing out. My current legislative director and deputy chief of staff is John Paul Paluskiewicz who put in many long nights preparing fifty individual amendments to a very flawed health care bill, and then stayed with me through long, late hours in the Rules Committee. Previous legislative directors have also provided significant guidance and I must mention Randi Reid and Josh Martin who previously filled that role. Stacy Defino and Matt Johnson previously helped me understand complicated legislative matters pertaining to energy legislation. I've been blessed with a very gifted group of individuals who have assisted me in the communications department: Lori McMahon, Michelle Stein, Alison Lynn, and most recently Lauren Bean. I have had very capable legislative counsels in Kim Reasoner, Sery Kim, James Decker, and George McCormick. Other staff members in Washington who have provided invaluable assistance included Amanda Stevens, Brenna Head, Ambyr Kinne, Rebecca West, Coleman Garrison, Blair Mixon, Jessica Strauss, Jessica Ngyuen-Trong, and Dr. Kim Stump M.D.

Staff in the district offices include district director Eric With, Janice Zimmerman, along with Melanie Torres, and Andrew Flores who work in constituent services. Joan Self has been staff assistant from the beginning. Robyn Vaughn oversees the business aspects of the district office as well as detailed attention to service academy nominees. Pat Bostic is my current director of development, and Faith Ellis previously filled that role. David Lehde provides invaluable help as director of District communications.

Current and past members of the Texas delegation to the United States House of Representatives have provided me significant help and guidance along the way. Our two senators, Kay Bailey Hutchison and John Cornyn have always been there to help when needed. Certainly my chairman and ranking member on the Committee Of Energy and Commerce, fellow Texan Joe Barton, showed a great deal of confidence in me when he chose me as the top Republican on the Subcommittee on Oversight and Investigations, and for that I will always be grateful.

I also will always be grateful to Sen. John McCain for making me one of the senior policy adviser's to the McCain/Palin campaign.

Newt and Callista Gingrich have been good friends during my brief tenure in Congress. Members of Newt's group, the Center for Health

Transformation, have also provided timely advice along the way. His staff at the Center has been extremely helpful to me, providing insight and information that otherwise might not have been available, so I'm extremely grateful to David Merritt, Jim Frogue and Michelle Stein (my former communications director, but worthy of mention again because she always told me that I should write a book).

Of course I shall always be grateful to the many patients and their families who trusted me with their care during my medical career, and now entrust me to represent them in the United States House of Representatives.

And finally to my grandson, Sebastian, who always seems to find a way to make me see the world in a way that had not occurred to me before. His unfailing attention to my continued education is clearly important, but his requirement that I always focus on the future and not the past is what I value most dearly.

NOTES

1 "Canadian doctors ask government for CDN$1 billion (US$765 million) to solve doctor-nurse shortage." AP Worldstream. 2004. *HighBeam Research*. (September 15, 2009). http://www.highbeam.com/doc/1P1-97830289.html

2 WorkPermit.com. "Canada - Alberta & Saskatchewan short of nurses and doctors." http://www.workpermit.com/news/2006_12_29/canada/nursing_doctor_shortage_alberta.htm.

3 Bales, Patrick. "Doctor shortage could jeopardize ER hours at Saugeen Memorial." *Shoreline Beacon*, 15 June 2009.

4 "No quick fix for MD shortage." Winnipeg Free Press. FP Canadian Newspapers Limited Partnership. 2007. *HighBeam Research*. 15 Sep. 2009 <http://www.highbeam.com>.

5 Skerritt, Jen. "Shortage affects surgeries, births." Winnipeg Free Press. 2008. *HighBeam Research*. (September 15, 2009). http://www.highbeam.com/doc/1P3-1596528121.html

6 O'Neill, Kathleen. "Is There a Doctor in the Area?" Energy Processing Canada. 2005. *HighBeam Research*. (September 15, 2009). http://www.highbeam.com/doc/1P3-995464621.html

7 Martin, Michelle. "Medical migration." Straight.com. http://www.straight.com/article-95157/medical-migration.

8 Khor, Martin. "Third World brain drain. (World Health Organization reports shortage of doctors)." Multinational Monitor. 2006. (September 15, 2009). http://www.highbeam.com/doc/1G1-154327771.html

9 http://www.investors.com/NewsAndAnalysis/SpecialReport.aspx?id=506106

10 Huntington, Samuel P. *The Clash of Civilization and the Remaking of World Order.* New York: Simon & Schuster, 1998.

11 Ibid.

12 Donnelly, Laura. "Public spending on 'nanny state' adverts rose 30-fold under Labour." *The Telegraph*, 28 August 2010.

13 Western Mail (Cardiff, Wales). 2009. *HighBeam Research*. (October 29, 2010). http://www.highbeam.com/doc/1G1-207763570.html

14 Annenberg Public Policy Center. "The 'Real' Uninsured." http://www.factcheck.org/2009/06/the-real-uninsured/.

15 CNN. "The CNN Democratic presidential debate in Texas." http://articles.cnn.com/2008-02-21/politics/debate.transcript_1_health-care-texas-candidates/23?_s=PM:POLITICS.

16 Ibid.

17 Nancy, Pelosi. Speech: 2010 Legislative Conference for the National Association of Counties. 9 March 2010

18 Sermo.com. "Senator Coburn MD (R. OK) Engages Physicians on Sermo to Guage Reaction to Healthcare Reform Bill." http://www.sermo.com/news/pr/03/march/4/senator-coburn-md-r-ok-engages-physicians-sermo-gauge-reaction-healthcare-reform-.

19 FoxNews.com. "Doctors Wage War Against Obama's Health Care Overhaul." http://www.foxnews.com/politics/2009/07/22/doctors-wage-war-obamas-health-care-overhaul/.

20 Ibid.

21 Connoly, Ceci, and Michael D. Shear. "In Televised Address, Obama Seeks to Calm Nation's Fears About Health-Care Reform." *Washington Post*, 23 July 2009.

22 "Dr. Obama's Tonsillectomy." *Wall Street Journal*, 26 July 2009.

23 "Letters" *Wall Street Journal*, 3 August 2009.

24 Ibid.

25 Obama, Barack. "Remarks by the President in Health Insurance Reform Town Hall." The White House. http://www.whitehouse.gov, 11 August, 2009

26 Cowan, Richard. "Pelosi lashes out against insurance companies." Reuters. http://www.reuters.com/article/idUSTRE56T4CZ20090730.

27 Ibid.

28 Hoff, John S. "The Public Health Insurance Option: Unfair Competition on a Tilting Field." Heritage Foundation. http://heritage.org/Research/Reports/2009/08/The-Public-Health-Insurance-Option-Unfair-Competition-on-a-Tilting-Field.

29 Carrol, Conn. "Still Not Convinced the Public Option is a Trojan Horse for Single-Payer?." Heritage Foundation. http://blog.heritage.org/?p=12248.

30 Ibid.

31 Ibid.

32 Obama, Barack. "President Obama's speech to American Medical Association." USA Today. http://www.usatoday.com/news/washington/2009-06-15-obama-speech-text_N.htm.

33 Heritage Foundation. "Medicare: Largest Denier of Health Care Claims."

http://blog.heritage.org/2009/10/06/medicare-largest-denier-of-health-care-claims/.

34   U.S. CARE OF CITIZENS IS 'SICKO'.(Editorial). Daily News (Los Angeles, CA). 2007. *HighBeam Research*. (November 4, 2010). http://www.highbeam.com/doc/1G1-164625761.html

35   Connecticut Health Insurance. "Shared Risk in Health Insurance." http://easyhealthins.com/blog/?p=34.

36   Ibid.

37   HealthReform.gov. "Insurance Companies Prosper, Families Suffer: Our Broken Health Insurance System." http://www.healthreform.gov/reports/insuranceprospers/insuranceprofits.pdf.

38   Tapper, Jake. "Sebelius Knocks Insurers for Big Profits and Big Rate Hikes." ABC News. http://blogs.abcnews.com/politicalpunch/2010/02/sebelius-knocks-insurers-for-big-profits-and-big-rate-hikes.html.

39   Miller, Sunlen. "Health Care Summit: Obama Calls for 'Spirit of Good Faith' Without 'Political Theater'." ABC News. http://blogs.abcnews.com/politicalpunch/2010/02/health-care-summit-obama-calls-for-the-spirit-of-good-faith-without-political-theater-.html.

40   Blendon RJ, Benson JM (April 2010). "Public opinion at the time of the vote on health care reform". *New England Journal of Medicine*. 362

41   Levin, Yuval. "At the Pleasure of the President." National Review Online. http://www.nationalreview.com/corner/249063/pleasure-president-yuval-levin.

42   Johnson, Avery. "Principal Financial Quits Writing Health-Care Policies." *Wall Street Journal*. http://online.wsj.com/article/SB10001424052748704789404575524281126700388.html.

43   CNN.com. "Obama: No reduced Medicare benefits in health care reform." http://articles.cnn.com/2009-07-28/politics/obama.health.care_1_medicare-advantage-medicare-trust-fund-medicare-benefits?_s=PM:POLITICS.

44   Weisman, Robert. "Harvard Pilgrim cancels Medicare Advantage plan." Boston.com. http://www.boston.com/business/healthcare/articles/2010/09/28/harvard_pilgrim_cancels_medicare_advantage_plan/.

45   Capretta, James Howard C. "Obamacare's Day of Reckoning." National Review Online. http://www.nationalreview.com/critical-condition/251820/obamacares-day-reckoning-james-c-capretta.

46   Book, Robert A., and James C. Capretta. "Reductions in Medicare Advantage Payments: The Impact on Seniors by Region." The Heritage Foundation. http://www.heritage.org/Research/Reports/2010/09/Reductions-in-Medicare-Advantage-Payments-The-Impact-on-Seniors-by-Region.

47   The page on the HHS site containing the speech transcript now has the following note: "Please note, this text has been updated as of Tuesday

October 5 to correct an error that was in the original remarks posted as prepared for delivery. We apologize for any confusion." http://www.hhs.gov/secretary/about/speeches/sp20101001.html

48 Haberkorn, Jennifer. "Department Of Health And Human Services errs on Medicare Advantage Read more: http://www.politico.com/news/stories/1010/43298.html#comments#ixzz14iEfxlO6." Politico.com.

49 lonso-Zaldivar, Ricardo. "HHS to insurers: Don't blame us for your rates." Associated Press. http://news.yahoo.com/s/ap/20100909/ap_on_bi_ge/us_health_insurance_warning.

50 Portnoy, Steven. "Sebelius: Time for 'Reeducation' on Obama Health Care Law." ABC News. http://blogs.abcnews.com/thenote/2010/08/sebelius-time-for-reeducation-on-obama-health-care-law.html?utm_source=twitterfeed&utm_medium=twitter.

51 Anonymous, . "Government Admits Medical Costs Will Rise Under Obamacare, Sebelius Threatens Insurers Who Criticize It, And Not Even Jon Stewart Is Buying The BS." The Blog Prof. http://theblogprof.blogspot.com/2010/09/government-admits-medical-costs-will.html.

52 Ivey, Steve. "Health reform, aging workers keep insurance premiums rising." Business First. http://www.bizjournals.com/louisville/print-edition/2010/10/22/health-reform-aging-workers-keep.html.

53 Families USA. "Lower Taxes, Lower Premiums: The New Health Insurance Tax Credit." http://www.familiesusa.org/assets/pdfs/health-reform/Premium-Tax-Credits.pdf.

54 Murdock, Deroy. "Obamacare: Condition Serious, Prognosis Grim. Obamacare is hiking, not cutting, costs." Congress.org. http://www.congress.org/congressorg/bio/userletter/?id=48778&letter_id=5958321501.

55 *The Wall Street Journal.* "Wyden Defects on Obamacare." http://online.wsj.com/article/SB10001424052748704206804575467592717163602.html#printMode.

56 Park, Gloria, and Fred Barbash. "Health Reform's Bureaucratic Spawn." Politico.com. http://www.politico.com/news/stories/0810/40561.html.

57 Joint Economic Committee: Republicans. "America's New Health Care System Revealed." http://jec.senate.gov/republicans/public/index.cfm?p=CommitteeNews&ContentRecord_id=bb302d88-3d0d-4424-8e33-3c5d2578c2b0.

58 Sowell, Thomas. BrainyQuote.com.

59 CaliforniaHealthline.org. "President Ties Health Care Reform to Economic Recovery." http://www.californiahealthline.org/Articles/2009/4/15/President-Ties-Health-Care-Reform-to-Economic-Recovery.aspx.

60 Pelosi, Nancy. "2010 Budget." Speaker.gov. http://www.speaker.gov/newsroom/legislation?id=0291.

61   Coburn, M.D., Tom, and John Barasso, M.D. "Grim Diagnosis: A Check-
     Up on the Federal Health Law."

62   Congressional Budget Office. "The Budget and Economic Outlook: An
     Update." http://www.cbo.gov/doc.cfm?index=11705.

63   Texas Health and Human Services Commission. "Impact on
     Health and Human Services Agencies." http://docs.google.com/
     viewer?a=v&q=cache:UF-1schq8iQJ:www.hhsc.state.tx.us/news/
     presentations/2010/HouseSelectFedHlthReformpdf+effect+of+health+care+r
     eform&hl=en&gl=us&pid=bl&srcid=ADGEEShWIF5R1Gp2l.

64   Sataline, Suzanne, and Shirley S. Wang. "Medical Schools Can't Keep Up."
     The Wall Street Journal. http://online.wsj.com/article/SB100014240527023
     04506904575180331528424238.html.

65   The Medicus Firm. "The Medicus Firm Physician Survey: Health Reform
     May Lead to Significant Reduction in Physician Workforce." http://www.
     themedicusfirm.com/pages/medicus-media-survey-reveals-impact-health-reform.

66   Ibid.

67   Jones, Terry. "45% Of Doctors Would Consider Quitting If Congress Passes
     Health Care Overhaul." Investors Business Daily. http://www.investors.
     com/newsandanalysis/article.aspx?id=506199.

68   http://www.annals.org/content/early/2010/08/23/0003-4819-153-8-
     201010190-00274.1.full

69   Dermondy, Cynthia, and Patricia Curtis. "41 Secrets Your Doctor Would
     Never Share." Reader's Digest, July 2010 http://www.rd.com/living-
     healthy/41-secrets-for-your-next-doctor-visit/article75920.html.

70   Ibid.

71   Oxentenko, MD, Amy S., Colin P. West, MD, Carol Popkave, MA, Steven
     E. Weinberger, MD, and Joseph C. Kolars, MD. "Time Spent on Clinical
     Documentation A Survey of Internal Medicine Residents and Program
     Directors." Archives of Internal Medicine. http://archinte.ama-assn.org/cgi/
     content/abstract/170/4/377.

72   Gilchrist, M.D., Valerie. "Physician Activities During Time Out of the
     Examination Room." Annals of Family Medicine. http://www.annfammed.
     org/cgi/content/abstract/3/6/494.

73   Signature MD. "Doctors Drowning in Paperwork." http://www.
     signaturemd.com/doctors-drowning-in-paperwork-concierge-medicine/.

74   Chen, MD, Lena M., Wildon R. Farwell, MD, and Ashish k. Jha, MD.
     "Primary Care Visit Duration and Quality." Archives of Internal Medicine.
     archinte.ama-assn.org/cgi/content/full/169/20/1866.

75   Ibid.

76   Op. cit. Dermondy, Reader's Digest

77   McQuillan, Lawrence J., and John R. Graham. "Doctors, patients need legal reform." Orange County Register. http://articles.ocregister.com/2010-09-08/opinion/24636581_1_medical-liability-doctors-health-care.

78   Bishop, MD, Tara F., Alex D. Federman, MD, and Salomeh Keyhani, MD. "Physicians' Views on Defensive Medicine: A National Survey." *Archives of Internal Medicine* 170, no. 12 (210): 1081–1083.

79   Lazar, Kay. "Doctors' fear of lawsuits tied to added costs of $1.4b." The Boston Globe, 18 November 2008.

80   Sakoulas, MD, George. "Relationship Between Population Density of Attorneys and Prevalence of Methicillin-Resistant Staphylococcus aureus: Is Medical-Legal Pressure on Physicians a Driving Force Behind the Development of An."*American Journal of Therapeutics* 16, no. 5 (2009)

81   Op. cit. Dermondy, *Reader's Digest.*

82   Ibid.

83   Palestrant, Daniel M.D., "Why Physicians Oppose the Health Care Reform Bill," *Sermo*, April 8, 2010.

84   The Physicians' Foundation. "The Physicians' Perspective: Medical Practice in 2008." http://www.physiciansfoundations.org/uploadedFiles/PF_Survey_Report_Nov08.pdf.

85   Ibid.

86   http://online.wsj.com/article/SB10001424052748704231304575091600470293066.html

87   Superliving.co.uk. "Take Responsibility for Your Own Health." https://www.superliving.co.uk/h/health-take-responsibility-for-your-own-health.html.

88   Op. cit. Dermondy, *Reader's Digest.*

89   Ibid.

90   Wachter, MD, Robert. "Primary care is more than just office visits." KevinMD.com. http://www.kevinmd.com/blog/2010/06/primary-care-office-visits.html.

91   Parkinson, MD, Jay. "Bureaucrats determine the business model of a doctor's practice." KevinMD.com. http://www.kevinmd.com/blog/2010/08/bureaucrats-determine-business-model-doctors-practice.html.

92   Palestrant, MD, Daniel. "CPT-Why physicians always get screwed, thanks AMA." Sermo.com. http://www.sermo.com/blog/2009/07/17/cpt-why-physicians-always-get-screwed-thanks-ama.

93   Ibid.

94   http://dyn.politico.com/printstory.cfm?uuid=D445B337-18FE-70B2-A801DC19D37EDF34

95   Gibbs, Robert. "Press Briefing by Press Secretary Robert Gibbs." WhiteHouse.gov. http://www.whitehouse.gov/the-press-office/briefing-white-house-press-secretary-robert-gibbs-42809.

96   Foster, Daniel. "The Democrats' Orvellian Talking Point." National
     Review Online. http://www.nationalreview.com/corner/195320/democrats-
     orwellian-talking-point/daniel-foster.

97   Pfeiffer, Dan. "Will the Republicans Post Their Health Plan . . .
     and When?." The White House Blog. http://www.whitehouse.gov/
     blog/2010/02/22/will-republicans-post-their-health-plan-and-when.

98   http://dyn.politico.com/printstory.cfm?uuid=9E55C1CA-18FE-70B2-
     A8AF3A94FAEF6235

99   McQuillan, Lawrence J., and John R. Graham. "Doctors, patients need legal
     reform." *Orange County Register*, 8 September 2010.

100 "The Association of Trial Lawyers of America—the 'home office' of Trial
     Lawyers Inc., routinely ranks among the top five PACs in federal campaign
     donations, leaning strongly to Democrats. In 2002, ATLA was the third
     most generous PAC, contributing $2.8 million; 89% of that money went to
     Democrats, making ATLA the largest PAC contributor to the Democratic
     party." Trial Lawyers Inc. "The Best Friends Money Can Buy." http://www.
     triallawyersinc.com/html/print10.html.

101 Wolf, Richard. "Doctors limit new Medicare patients." USA Today. http://
     www.usatoday.com/news/washington/2010-06-20-medicare_N.htm.

102 Ibid.

103 Morrisey, Ed. "Shocker: Doctors taking fewer Medicare patients." HotAir.
     com. http://hotair.com/archives/2010/06/21/shocker-doctors-taking-fewer-
     medicare-patients/.

104 The 8,011-Person Crisis: Obama's pre-existing condition program is a bust."
     The Wall Street Journal, 12 November 2010. http://online.wsj.com/article/
     SB10001424052748703805004575606891744060162.html.

105 Frost & Sullivan. "Frost & Sullivan: Wellness A Critical Factor for Healthy
     Corporate Wealth." http://www.frost.com/prod/servlet/press-release.
     pag?docid=201485316.

106 Rohack, MD, J. James. "Congress Delays Medicare Physician Payment Cut
     Again to June 1." American Medical Association: News. http://www.ama-
     assn.org/ama/pub/news/news/medicare-cut-delayed-june.shtml.

107 Worth, Tammy. "Agencies warn of coming doctor shortage." *The Los Angeles
     Times*, 7 June 2010. http://articles.latimes.com/2010/jun/07/health/la-he-
     doctor-shortage-20100607.

INDEX